THE EMPOWERED ENTREPRENEUR

mastering the art of a thriving business

Elizabeth Cairns

THE EMPOWERED ENTREPRENEUR

mastering the art of a thriving business

Elizabeth Cairns

CERATO

DEDICATION

For Monkey, a true master, my inspiration and best friend. x

Author Elizabeth Cairns

Editor Michael Cairns

Creative Direction & Design Fiona Humberstone

Illustration Gail Jones

Photography Annie Spratt, Cathy Pyle, Cecelina Tornberg, Elizabeth Cairns, Fiona Humberstone, Katie Spicer

MIX
Paper from responsible sources
FSC® C124385

CONTENTS

INTRODUCTION

There is something deeply empowering about running a business on your terms, one that plays to your unique strengths and engages your passions.

There is something transformative about living a life that is aligned with what really matters and bringing that into your work in a meaningful way.

When you are an Empowered Entrepreneur, you can be brave and make choices that open doors, move you in the direction of your dreams and get a taste of what it's like to fulfil your creative potential.

Everything you need to run a thriving business and live an inspired life is inside you. *The Empowered Entrepreneur* is a book written to reveal that brilliance, help you make it real, remind you what you're really capable of, and let your awesomeness loose on the world.

We are living in an age where the trade-off for a successful business is our wellbeing. The cost of achieving our commercial goals is time with our loved ones, whilst our sanity is held ransom by so many external demands.

The pace of life has been quickening dramatically in recent years, spurred on by developments in technology and the birth of social media. The anxiety created by the constant struggle to keep up, to be current, to *make* more, to *have* more, to *be* more, to have the Pinterest-perfect life, is driving us all mad.

Corporations are expecting more and more of their workforce too, and give less and less in return. We are all over scheduled and there is a frenzy of 'busy' that, for some, is still considered a measure of success. For those who have jumped off the corporate bandwagon to run their own enterprises, it comes with a hell of a hangover. A way of working that resembles the nose to the grindstone work ethic or work-hard play-hard mindset so typical of much of corporate life. So much of what we unconsciously consider as successful, of what we should be doing, thinking, consuming, creating, is fed to us by the media and society at large. No time to think, no thought to question, no space to breathe. There is little room to move on the bus, let alone get off and choose a different ride.

Well, no more! Change is coming and you are at the forefront of a tribe of trailblazers forging a new way of working in the world. One that successfully marries commercial success with purposeful work and prioritises those things that matter to you. Not least your health, happiness and a worthwhile life of meaning.

This book will put the power back in your hands and inspire you to create work that is, however big or small, both meaningful, manageable and wholly successful. I want you to know that you don't have to wait until you retire; achieve your goals; earn that 'x' figure income… to enjoy life at a pace that works for *you*. This isn't about chasing a dream, it's about living it, every day. This book will help you become the conscious creator of the life you want to live and run a business your own way, with your unique gifts and talents at its heart.

You may be wondering how I came to be writing this book. My approach is not as a marketing or business expert, although I've been around the block. Nor as a literary graduate, although I've always been a writer. Primarily I offer it as someone who knows people. *Really* knows them, and has studied them up close and personal for a very long time. What makes them tick, what holds them back. What shifts limiting paradigms and unleashes potential and how all of that comes into play in the arena of our work.

I have an uncommon perspective to share, one that comes from experience in two very different worlds.

I started in corporate life early, one of the benefits of skipping the university part, and at the same time as building my career in the real world, I immersed myself in the more alternative arena of complementary health. I trained and practiced first as an holistic therapist in various disciplines: massage, aromatherapy, reflexology. As my personal meditation and yoga practice deepened over the years, I extended my study to the more esoteric fields of energy work. Along-side my day job, I built a thriving therapy practice working one to one and with small groups.

My passion for psychology and the body mind connection was liberally applied to both my parallel careers with gusto.

There came a time when I could ignore the pull no longer and I decided to go my own way. When I left formal employment in the corporate world and became a fledgeling entrepreneur I gave myself permission to say 'yes'. Yes to anything that inspired me, excited me or challenged me. That opened doors I never would have thought possible, had I stayed in the confines of my safe and predictable corporate existence.

I had incredible experiences that have shaped my thinking, informed my perspective and broadened my appreciation for what it means to truly thrive. I worked with masters in their field and those at the top of their game, all the while observing closely, listening, learning.

I discovered a passion for creating and facilitating team development programmes for corporates and, now on the other side of the fishbowl, I could see more clearly. As well as supporting SME's, speaking and coaching, I was invited to coach and train with leaders in FTSE 100 companies and others from around the globe. I got up close and personal with what it takes to make teams and businesses truly high performing.

Still with one foot firmly in a Birkenstock, I ran holistic personal and spiritual development retreats several times a year in inspiring places of wild and natural beauty. Working deeply with individuals seeking to make positive change in their lives and those of others. It was here I became intimate with what it is to live wholeheartedly in the world and live a life of meaning.

Over these past 18 years of working with entrepreneurs and teams from all over the world, I have seen people become slaves to their work in a way that douses the fires of passion, cripples the spirit and drains the mojo of even the most dynamic of creatives. I have longed to find a way to help these bright and brilliant souls reclaim what is theirs; the joy, vitality and inspiration that comes with running an authentic, thriving business.

I hope this book will challenge you to think differently, to put vitality, inspiration and creativity at the heart of what you do, and invite you to step into what's possible when you live the life of an Empowered Entrepreneur.

WHO IS THIS BOOK FOR?

If you'd rather be a free thinker, go your own way and create a business that works on your terms, than blindly follow the herd, this book is for you.

If you know there has to be a better way of working than slaving away with little joy for little reward, but perhaps haven't found it yet, this book is for you. If you long to do your best work, to be inspired, to create and to do work with purpose and meaning, this was written for you. If you long to manage your business in a way that supports and enhances your life rather than constantly compromising, chasing your tail or trading your wellbeing, read on.

For any entrepreneur, no matter what stage of your business journey, there will be something for you in these pages. We can all benefit from working in a more considered, empowered way, having more flexibility and creating more opportunities.

If you apply what you'll learn here, you can enjoy being more confident in your choices for your business, clear in your criteria for effective decision making. You can say yes to the right things and enjoy the certainty of knowing what to walk away from. You will have a greater understanding of how vitality and inspiration work in your business and how to harness them for greater success and fulfilment. You will explore new ways of working to enhance productivity and avoid the challenges of overwhelm, overwork or avoidance.

There are always opportunities to work smarter. With this book you can streamline to create the most elegant, efficient and profitable way of working.

You can find deeper meaning in what you do and take your work to greater levels of mastery and satisfaction.

Being an Empowered Entrepreneur is about taking ownership of your business and running with ideas in your own way so I've deliberately not included case studies and kept the step-by-step how-to's to a minimum. You can find stories and podcasts from fellow entrepreneurs on the website to inspire you, but remember the best approach for your unique business will stem from *you*.

This book has been designed to act as a catalyst for you and a spring-board for growth and development.

I urge you to take some action, however small and apply what you learn. Experiment. If you want to work through the chapters in order, step by step then great. If you'd rather flick through, pick a page and start there, knock yourself out. However you approach it, I guarantee you will gain so much more if you take action, and have fun doing it.

your book, your way

HOW TO USE THIS BOOK

That said, I also hope this book will be something to savour and ponder on, a companion on your journey to help deepen your experience of yourself and your work. Change doesn't happen over night. Be gentle with yourself. Know that wherever you are is exactly where you need to be and that it's a great place to begin an adventure. The Empowered Entrepreneur has been a true labour of love and a long time in the nurturing, so above all, I hope you enjoy it and find inspiration in its pages.

'Tell me, what is it you plan
to do with your one
wild and precious life?'

MARY OLIVER

LIVE WITH INTENTION, GO YOUR OWN WAY

Life is wild and precious, short and unpredictable. As an entrepreneur you've already chosen not to settle for the mundane, for the ordinary. When you are empowered, you are master of your own destiny and can shape your future. You can actively create the extraordinary.

To become empowered is to understand that you have choice and can live and work with intention. When you live and work in this way, everything changes. You are liberated to pursue what matters most, you are emancipated to forge your own unique way of working, you are free to take your creativity, innovation, and leadership to new heights.

Engaging with life in this way is the hallmark of an Empowered Entrepreneur. It begins with recognising that you *do* have power.

Once you know that, in your bones, then you can exercise it, in the little things and the big things. You can challenge assumptions and conventions until forging your own trail becomes second nature.

When you make that choice to live and work with intention, you are free. You are not at the mercy of trends or misguided by the strong opinions of others. You know your own heart and mind, and are brave enough to follow where they lead. Empowered Entrepreneurship calls you to innovate. This innovation isn't confined just to your physical products or your content, but also your approach and how you operate behind the scenes of your business.

Part of being an Empowered Entrepreneur then, is to have the courage to define your own terms. To create a business that really works for you. To find new and innovative ways to do the work that you love and to do it to the best of your ability.

When you live as an Empowered Entrepreneur, you know that what you do makes a difference, that your thoughts, your actions and your attitudes shape your experience and that of your audience, and you live this truth every single day.

When you decide to consciously create the life you want to live, it's transformative. You don't just fit your job around things or fit your life around your work, you don't settle. You create a life worth living. You take hold of the reins and damn well enjoy the ride.

VITALITY

the sustaining force of your business

Wild rose: connects us to the joy
and adventure of life

VITALITY

the sustaining force of your business

There is an energy that, when you harness it, can elevate and propel your business beyond what you might have thought possible. An energy that requires comparatively little effort to create and yet is nourishing, self sustaining and life affirming. It enables you to work hard, without it feeling like hard work. It accelerates things without you ever feeling rushed. It facilitates joy, energy and passion and opens the way for inspiration.

Vitality, the force that you must work on creating, raising and maintaining if you are to fulfil your potential and create a sustainable, viable business.

An abundance of vitality not only facilitates your wellbeing but super-charges the endeavours of a creative entrepreneur.

Vitality can be measured in the amount of energy you have, in the overall state of your health, in the flow of your creative ideas and, as an entrepreneur, the success of your business.

When you don't have it, you have little drive, just going through the motions, connecting superficially with life, and your business moves at a sluggish pace. Worse, you may become sick, lose motivation and inspiration all together and your business goes nowhere.

Vitality is abundant in nature, generated in the body, affected by the mind and your environment. Abundant vitality is your birthright, your natural state of being. Everything within you is geared up to seek and operate from this easy, efficient and enjoyable state.

RAISING VITALITY
your first priority

To connect with this wonderful energy, you just need to get out of the way, recognise what inhibits your vitality and what feeds it and make nurturing it a priority. In this chapter we will explore the basics and the subtleties of nurturing your vital energy and where to start if you want to shift some of those blockers.

If you want a successful sustainable business and a healthy and meaningful life, maintaining optimum vitality is your essential first priority as an Empowered Entrepreneur. Not the bottom line, not your to-do list, and definitely not your social media stats! Without vitality there's no fuel for growth. There's no energy for action. There's no kindling of magic.

Vitality and inspiration are dancing partners, both pivotal forces for your successful business. They work together to keep things moving, to aid creation and open the doors to possibility. Vital energy opens the channels for inspiration to flow and inspiration shows us where to take that energy and put it to good work.

NURTURING VITALITY
taking care of the basics

To nurture your vitality you need to take care of the basics first and the basics begin with your body. An Empowered Entrepreneur takes their physical wellbeing seriously and recognises the link between that and a sustainable business.

To thrive, your body needs to be taken care of. Not in the way you might take care of an old second hand car you're not that fond of, running it into the ground as just a box for getting around in. It needs the kind of care and attention you might give a young child: It needs to be listened to, nourished with good nutrition, kept hydrated, given plenty of good-quality undisturbed sleep, daily movement, fresh air, sunlight and exercise, appropriate sensory stimulation, loving touch, safe attachments... you get the idea.

The basics are so often ignored though. They drop down the priority list in favour of more lofty pursuits, or when we are pushing a deadline, or when life just gets too busy. We forget to drink water and, in an effort to keep going, we top up on caffeine instead. We stay on the screen late into the evening and suffer disrupted sleep. We skip the exercise class because we think we don't have time. It's easy to get into the carb-crash cycle of eating fast-prepared food at our desk or skipping meals altogether because it's too much of a faff to stop and prepare a decent, well-balanced meal. Lucky for us, the body is extremely resourceful and adaptable, capable of taking a serious amount of bashing before it's beat. But that doesn't mean it should.

An Empowered Entrepreneur prioritises their wellbeing. If you want to create the conditions for optimum vitality, to realise your dreams and aspirations, then you can't skip the basics.

DESIGNING YOUR DAY WITH VITALITY IN MIND

To make vitality a priority and create the optimum conditions for it to grow, it needs to be built seamlessly into your every day. It needs to become habit. You need to enjoy the benefits, take opportunities to nurture it and plan with vitality in mind.

Imagine you were designing an ideal working day for you and your best friend, with vitality as the priority. What would it look like, what would you include?

Your primary responsibility is making sure your friend is well cared for, has everything they need to be physically and emotionally happy, ends their day feeling better, and wanting to do it all over again.

If it was me, there would definitely be some lovely food, really luscious, nutritious feast-for-the-senses food that was a joy to eat. There would be time for a walk in nature, to think, to move, to enjoy the weather. There would be time to be creative, to play, to use our hands. There would be time to get stuck in and have that lovely feeling of satisfaction that comes from achieving a goal through doing productive work. There would be time to rest and restore. I'd speak to them kindly, I'd offer them regular refreshments and comfort breaks. I'd give them a regular change of scene and provide stimulation for mind, body and soul. We'd have a laugh and we'd want to come back the next day for more.

Imagine now if that person shared the usual experience of your average working day instead. They could only eat, drink and rest when you did, were only active when you were, and did everything that you do on a typical working day. How would their experience be different? Would they come away feeling nurtured, treasured and energised? Would they want to come back the following day and do it all over again?

Notice what insights you get from this simple exercise. What would you change in relation to your daily working and nurturing habits? How could you take better care of your body in particular as you go about your daily routine?

BACK TO BASICS - BACK TO BED

Sleep is the secret weapon of the high vitality entrepreneur. Little talked about, fairly unglamorous, but totally game changing. If you want optimum vitality and a high performing brain, you need to preserve your sleep and get what your body needs each night.

Without going into all the research, it's generally accepted that getting to sleep before 10pm yields considerably more benefits than staying up later, and most people need between seven and nine hours a night for optimum functioning.

Getting to sleep and staying asleep can be challenging for many creative entrepreneurs. All those ideas buzzing around, and all that excess adrenaline from burning the candle at both ends, can get in the way.

Focusing on shifting your sleep pattern to one that is brain friendly and gets you the restorative sleep you need to be at your best is fairly straight forward and begins with the decision to make it a priority.

A lovely way to begin to do this is to make your bedroom a sanctuary for sleep. You can create a truly wonderful haven of tranquility and restoration with very little effort.

Avoid bright lighting, have subtle or neutral wall colourings or those with blue or green rather than red hues as they are more calming for the body. Keep the temperature on the cool side, use a fan if you need to. Treat yourself to wonderful bedding that makes you want to sink into bed and feels soothing to your skin. Keep screens firmly out of the bedroom. Don't use your phone as an alarm clock but rather a grow clock that helps you wake more naturally or a traditional alarm. Keep the bedroom clear and free from clutter or distraction or anything that reminds you of everything you need to do. You should be able to walk across the threshold and switch off. Experiment with the position of your bed to find the perfect spot that helps you feel most at ease. Introduce house plants to provide a calming aesthetic of the mind and purify your space. Ivy and spider plants in particular are thought to be helpful in improving air quality.

SLEEP: HOW TO ENJOY MORE OF THE GOOD STUFF

If you'd like to enjoy deeper, longer, more restorative sleep in your
new haven of rest try any or all of these:

Getting to bed before 10pm daily.

*No screens, preferably an hour before
sleep* and consider using a night mode
early evening which reduces back light if
you do find you need to work.

Avoiding stimulants in the late
afternoon and evening, particularly
caffeine and sugar.

Eat on the light side in the evening
and avoid anything too rich or salty as
if your body is struggling to stay
hydrated over night it will affect your
quality of sleep.

Stay well hydrated during the day.

Take five minutes to journal or free
write to clear the mind before bed.

Avoid stimulating exercise in the
evening. Keep the high octane workouts
for the morning and switch for a
restorative yoga class instead.

Enjoy a really warm Epsom salts bath
going straight to bed afterwards. The
salts begins to relax the muscles and as
you cool down from your bath you will
find it easier to drift off to sleep.

Keep a note pad and pen by the bedside
to capture any thoughts that drive you
nuts and keep you awake.

Try the Bach Flower Essences of White
Chestnut, for circling thoughts, or
Olive for tiredness, they can both help
with sleep.

Get a regular massage and train your
body to deeply relax.

Take up a regular meditation habit and
gain a little more control of your mind.

WATER
the vitality elixir

The fastest way to improve your short term energy and overall vitality? Drink water. Slumps in energy and mental performance are so often due to dehydration but we rarely make the link. Drinking enough water helps raise the vitality of the body in so many essential ways from clearing toxins to hydrating the insulating sheaths around our nerve cells for a more effective brain. Every function in your body requires water and with around 70% of you made from the stuff your health is dependant on it. It is estimated that an adult body loses over two litres (80 ounces) of water a day through respiration, sweating and detoxifying. So drinking less than that amount will seriously compromise on brain function and skin health in particular.

You may think you don't need to drink much water because you don't feel thirsty, but start giving the body more of what it really needs and you'll notice so many benefits you won't want to stop. This comes with a caveat though. Too much, particularly in one go, can affect your mineral balance so don't go crazy. 2.5 litres a day spread out in manageable amounts is plenty for the average person in normal temperatures, not overly exerting themselves.

WATER: MAKING IT EASY TO DRINK

Make it easy for yourself to drink so it becomes second nature.

Have a full glass by your bed and drink one upon waking.

Instead of dehydrating coffee first thing *try hot water and lemon* for greater hydration.

Set up little reminders to drink Pair it with other activities you don't have to think about and it will soon become habit. Every time you sit down at your desk make sure your water glass is full and then be sure to finish it before you get up again.

Treat yourself to a beautiful water jug and glass Fill it each morning with fresh water, a slice of lemon, lime, mint, cucumber, whatever takes your fancy and put it somewhere in view. Enjoy throughout the day.

If you like regular routine, *set a timer for every hour* as a reminder to drink a full glass.

However you increase your water intake you will soon be enjoying the benefits: enhanced focus and concentration, better mood, faster reaction times, improved sleep, clarity of mind and memory to name just a few.

DOING VITAL WORK
maintaining vitality in your working day

The way you spend your time affects your vitality. More vitality is good for business, and good for you. Anything that drains your energy will get in the way of you doing your best work. Anything that kills your inspiration will hinder your business growth. Anything that creates tension or slows momentum makes running your business more difficult.

What way of working would you create if you could?

As an Empowered Entrepreneur you can shape your business in *any way you choose*. You're not bound by convention. You can learn and take inspiration from what others have done, whilst maintaining the freedom of your unique direction. You can be aware of trends without being a slave to them. You can notice what your competitors are doing and not be pulled off track, because you trust your own instincts. You can liberate yourself, go your own way.

Choosing to shape your business in a way that truly works for you, that creates vitality, harnesses inspiration and puts your unique gifts and talents at its heart makes all the difference. Your business instantly becomes more sustainable, more authentic - and makes more commercial sense. Not to mention, so much more enjoyable.

First, you need to consider the bigger picture of work you have chosen to do, the offerings at the heart of your business. I believe that to be truly successful, and we will explore what that means for you in more detail later, you need to be doing work that inspires, excites and captivates you, and raises your energy.

When you have found that work, you then need to consider your approach to it and creating a structure that enables you to deliver your offering in the most empowered way possible.

We'll look at the bigger picture later in *The Work*, but for now, with our focus on raising our vitality, let's get a little more granular.

PRIORITISING VITALITY WITHIN YOUR WORK

Let's look at what you do in your business everyday. There is work that will boost your vitality and jobs that will drain it dry. The ideal is to work in an energy efficient way, to do more of what raises your vitality and less of what drains it.

You probably already have a fairly good sense of which things fall into which camp, now let's get some real clarity and start making improvements.

List out all the parts of running a business that you love, for whatever reason. Those things that are easy, or challenging in a rewarding way. Things you don't put off and that you get excited about. Those elements that are meaningful.

Create a second list of all those tasks, however big or small *that feel like a chore.* Anything you dread, procrastinate over, avoid. Anything that makes you cross, grumpy, overly anxious or bored. Anything that bugs you, takes more time than it should or irritates you for whatever reason.

Write a third list of *anything you're not currently doing but would like to be,* because you want to, not because you feel you should.

Assessing the energy cost

OK, so just to help with motivation a little, let's look at the cost to your business of wading through all that dross, fighting fires, managing admin or any of those other vitality-sapping tasks. How much of your time and energy do you spend on things on the second list? Don't worry if you're not sure, take a guess.

If you want to find out for sure, keep a task log for a week. Write down everything you do in your working day and give it an energy rating between one and ten. Anything below five is a drainer, anything between five and seven is neutral and anything eight and above raises energy.

How much of your time at work each day, each week, is spent engaged in those things that *raise your vitality, feed your inspiration and create meaningful work* that adds value?

Spending time wisely

Now you understand what's sustaining and what's draining you, to create a new way of working and shift the emphasis towards higher vitality, you need to spend the highest proportion of your time and energy in your business on things that fall into list one.

To deal with list two you just need to dig a little deeper and be a little creative. Take another look at list two, the energy sapping chores.

What on this list are you doing not because you love doing it but because you *think you have to or feel you should?*

Now give yourself permission to *challenge the assumption* that they need doing in the first place. *Really* challenge it. Who says it needs to be this way? What's the benefit of this particular task for you and your business? Is there one?

CURATING YOUR WORKLOAD

To review and streamline those energy sapping tasks, ask yourself...

Can I drop it altogether?

Does it really have to be done? How do I know this is really important, who says so? Perhaps you're a personal stylist, for example, who loves working with people on styling their image. If you can't stand shopping, is there any reason to make personal shopping part of your offering just because every other stylist does it?

Perhaps you're a florist but have a family and value time with them at the weekend. If packing a van in the small hours, schlepping about the country and spending all day on your feet destroys your will to live, don't assume you have to be doing wedding floristry just because so many other florists offer it. It's your business, you can shape it any way you want to. Play to your strengths, be creative around what you can offer across different markets.

You can take your business in any direction that inspires you. When you shape it according to how doing the work affects your energy, it will make a huge difference.

Can I delegate it?

Are you making the assumption that because it's your business, you have to be the one to do it? Not so. There are huge benefits to outsourcing those tasks that demotivate you, are overly hard work, or you're just not that skilled at.

What would you outsource if you could? Even if you think your business can't afford it, the cost of you being uninspired or overworked and on your knees is far too high a price to pay if you want to create a sustainable business capable of growth.

Can I streamline it?

If it's something that happens repeatedly in your business, sending invoices or handling enquiries for example, then you can either automate it, or have a very efficient process for dealing with it. We will look at this in more detail in *Getting It Done*.

Can I achieve the same result in a different way?

I've met countless entrepreneurs who are hell-bent on having a newsletter, even though they can't stand writing, because someone has told them they need one. They dread doing it, so they put it off and therefore do it inconsistently, if at all. A newsletter is a means to an end, not always the end in itself.

Think about the end goal. What is it you're hoping to achieve? Showing your expertise, engaging with an audience, building a loyal following? All great advantages of a newsletter, but how else could you achieve that end? If you love to write, and you enjoy having a platform to share your thoughts, your images, to add value or just to have a voice then great, go for it! If not, find another way. This is about challenging the assumptions you might be making about the things that drain your energy, and not just following the herd. When you free up the time spent on those things that aren't your forte, you can channel it more effectively into activities that will actually grow your business. If your focus is on the right things you will be more consistent, more able to do your best work, more likely to shine and create that all important buzz around what you do that attracts attention.

Can I change the way I feel about it?
If you're convinced you're not just following the herd and you do actually need to do something you're not that fond of, you always have the choice to shift how you feel about it. An Empowered Entrepreneur doesn't settle for just slogging on through. You act with purpose, for a reason.

One powerful way to shift your perspective on something is to go value hunting. Ask yourself what's important about a particular task. What does it enable? What are all the benefits to you, to the business, to others, of doing it? And then keep asking the question of what's important about each subsequent answer you get until you hit on something that makes it feel more worthwhile. Heck, you can change the way you feel about ironing with this simple trick.

Sometimes you can shift how you feel about a task simply by making sure you are paid well enough for it. I know

that if I'm going to spend a whole day away from my family, with all the other associated costs and logistics that entails, then it needs to be both work I love to do and make good sense financially, otherwise it's too easy for me to get resentful and demotivated. If it's client-facing work that you're looking at, are you charging enough for it to feel worthwhile?

This isn't about removing every possible thing that makes you feel a little bit low. Not everything you have to do in your business will have you singing from the hills. Some contrast is necessary so you can really appreciate the good stuff and there is benefit in working through things that are tricky and uncomfortable.

It's about making intentional choices, between those things that are creating energy, feeding your soul and growing your business and those things that aren't quite so pleasurable.

It's a way of shaping your daily life so that it works for you and makes the business of doing business less of a drag and more of a delight.

SETTING YOUR HOURS
getting time on your side

Let's consider the overall structure of your working day. For many of us in business we fall into working patterns just because it's expected, because we carry old habits from previous employment with us when we start up, or simply because there's so much to get done.

Does 9-5 sound like a dream because the reality looks more like 7-7? Do you currently work weekends to get through the to-do list? Has working through lunch, or working late into the night become the norm? Do you begin and end your day checking emails, allowing it to creep into family time or nights out with friends? Are *real* holidays a distant memory or considered a dream? Are you constantly busy but not always as productive as you'd like? Have you forgotten what it feels like to really 'switch off'? Most driven entrepreneurs I meet can relate to one if not all of the above.

Whether you feel the pressure of time so acutely or not, I invite you to deliberately choose the hours you want to work rather than feeling pigeon-holed into a 9-5 or a five day week just because it's the perceived norm.

When in the year do you want to work and when would you like a break? Would you benefit from a few weeks out spread out across the year? Do you want to keep school holidays free to spend with the family? How many days a week, a month, a year would you like to work and in what blocks? How many hours of those days would you like to work and is it different on different days? If you could wave a magic wand and put any schedule in place what would it be?

If you start from that point, and structure everything else in your business around it, it is totally game-changing. It will, of course, affect what you need to charge, how you structure your offerings and whether you might need to grow the personnel side of your business or adjust deadlines, but where there's a will, there's always a way.

A year ago if you had asked a dear friend of mine what she thought of moving to a four day work week whilst maintaining, if not increasing, her revenue, she would have never entertained the possibility. That same friend currently enjoys every Friday and weekend off and a much more sustainable business. How? Because she dared to entertain the possibility and give herself permission to make it work. She worked through what it would take for that to be possible.

She reassessed some of the assumptions she was making about her work and the way she had to approach it and voila...goodbye burnout, hello spa break.

WORKING WITH YOUR BODY NOT AGAINST IT

Choosing working hours that make the most of your own periods of high vitality makes sense too. If you're one of the 20% of people on the planet who are a night owl, and welcome a slow and steady start, for example, it doesn't make sense to front load your critical and creative work to the early hours of the day. Likewise if you've had a period of illness, high stress or it feels like burnout is just around the corner, you might want to make some drastic changes in the short term to redress the vitality balance before you are able to work at the pace you might like.

It makes sense to structure your day in accordance with your natural bio-rhythms. For most of us non night-owls, you will begin the day with a peak of energy and mood, it will dip significantly early afternoon and then recover again toward the end of the day. Scheduling tasks that require high focus, mental clarity and strategic thinking make most sense during the initial peak. Routine admin tasks, like email, should be deferred until after lunch when the trough hits, and tasks that benefit from more free thinking like brainstorming, work well later in the day when the mind is alert but more free thinking. If working in line with your body's natural rhythm is something that interests you, then you'll find a wealth of further information, supported by rigorous empirical evidence, in Daniel Pink's book *When - The scientific secrets of perfect timing*.

Whatever changes you make to the structure of your working day it may help to bear in mind that it doesn't have to be permanent. Nothing is set in stone unless you want it to be. You can give yourself permission to experiment, to try new approaches and to go with something that works for now, and review it again in the future. The point is, you have *choice*.

STAYING INSPIRED

inspiration as a daily practice

If your vitality is what powers your business as an Empowered Entrepreneur, your inspiration is what leads it. Your inspiration feeds your business with the ideas, motivation, and innovation it needs to survive and thrive. You do your best work when you are inspired, in flow and in a state of high natural vitality.

The task of getting and staying inspired is the work that comes before the creative work itself. Once it has you in its thrall, inspiration weaves a singular magic, but it can be a fickle companion.

How many times have you gone to a workshop or spent time with friends and felt lifted, motivated, determined to tackle business anew, only to find a while later that your motivation has curled up and gone back into stubborn hibernation?

There's almost an unacknowledged expectation that once you've been imbued with that magical get-up-and-go that it should be with you ad-infinitum. So the realisation that it's got-up-and-gone can often leave you feeling worse than before. Particularly if you have an important project you want to bring to life or are relying on it to grow your business.

At times like these you need to remember that tapping into the flow of inspiration is a daily practice, not a one hit wonder. Whilst wonderful adventures in self development can bring you the necessary paradigm shifts to take you to new levels of thinking and being, what it comes down to in the end is making inspiration a daily choice. When you take ownership of your own state of flow and creativity, the pursuit of inspiration can become a joyful obsession.

I once heard someone say that inspiration is a bit like bathing and I'm inclined to agree. The effect of it wears off after a while and you need to get back in the bath.

Inspiration isn't just something for the chosen few, it's available in spades to anyone who goes looking for it. As an Empowered Entrepreneur, finding inspiration is not something that you leave to chance, it's something that you can create the conditions for and seek out with wanton enthusiasm.

vitality

CREATING THE CONDITIONS FOR INSPIRATION

Let's start to create the conditions for the seeds of inspiration to grow in your business. There's a few things to bear in mind before you begin:

To be inspired is simply a choice to see the world through a difference lens, one that looks for opportunity, possibility, creativity and inspiration. When you make a decision to seek inspiration you can't help but find it. It affects the way you experience everything, and completely changes the nature of the game.

It is greatly helped by curiosity and a sense of wonder If you can practice getting into these states they often lead to inspiration. Not sure how to do it? Go and spend a few hours with a toddler in the woods and get into their world, they'll soon show you how it's done.

Seeking inspiration is done via all the senses There's no need to limit yourself to the one or two you feel most comfortable in. Using multiple senses wakes up more areas of the brain, creates more connections, and makes living a whole body experience.

Look outside of your chosen field If you're only looking at others in your niche on Instagram or Pinterest for example, you're missing an opportunity and it's unlikely you'll be feeding your unique inspiration. Consider exploring architecture, fashion, literature, fine art, modern art, interiors, the options are endless, and move away from screen based inspiration when you can.

It's much easier to be inspired when you are actively part of the experience than when you are just observing. Watching, seeing with new eyes and observing are all key of course, but if you can maintain a connected quality of presence and allow what you are seeing to move you, it's even more powerful. Real life rather than virtual/online experiences are often much more inspiring.

INSPIRATION: WHERE TO FIND IT

Inspiration can be found anywhere. You don't have to do anything particularly dramatic, although of course you can, and you don't have to make drastic changes to harness it. It's more of a mindset and a way of interacting with the world you're already in as well as an opportunity to get out there and experiment.

It doesn't have to take long. You can absolutely create fully immersive inspiring experiences that last hours or days for yourself and I wholeheartedly recommend that you do, but it can also be found in the little things and the fleeting moments. You just need to be awake to it.

The activity of being inspired builds inspiration muscle and gets faster over time. With practice you will recognise the state and how that feels in your body mind and soul and be able to turn it on at will.

For inspiration to work for your business you have to allow it to lead you, it requires action to build the momentum so you need to allow space to follow that lead. We'll talk more about creating that space in the next chapter.

Now we have a sense of some of the fundamentals let's get to it.

What inspires you?
We can begin with what you already know. What inspires you at the moment?

Which environments give you that lift? What or who creates that ripple effect of energy and ideas? What gets your skin tingling and your mind buzzing?

Make a quick list of at least 30 people, places or activities that inspire you. Opposite you'll find a few of mine if you need ideas: The list goes on and on and on…

Listening to an expert in their field talk about their subject with passion...Thank you Ted Talks! *Going to a new restaurant and trying their tasting menu* Kew Gardens *Singing workshops with improvisation* Smelling my way around my garden *Watching and hearing a master drummer, luckily I live with one* Yoga with a wonderful teacher *Watching a potter throwing a pot* Beautiful spaces *A well laid out grazing table* The dark Peak District at night, hello Milky Way *Being in a room with people smarter than me, easily done ;)* Flicking through a good recipe book *Rituals and ceremony, either watching or taking part - like making Turkish coffee or a winter fire ceremony* Wild camping *Meditation* Heading into the woods with my camera or spending time with a passionate photographer *Hearing and seeing beautiful live music played/sung well* Barefoot walking *Learning something new... anything* Dipping into a good book, non fiction works best for me *Dancing, the kind where you can really let it all go like 5 rhythms or Sufi Whirling* Following a forager through the woods *Taking a shower - yes really, all the best ideas start there.*

INSPIRATION: WHEN WOULD YOU LIKE IT?

Where in your day does it makes sense to trigger inspiration?

For me it's either right at the start so the energy carries me through the day or around mid afternoon when I need a little lift. Better still, both.

Front-loading inspiration into your working day can make an incredible difference. Particularly if you combine it with something that naturally raises your vitality: A brisk walk while listening to a podcast; a spot of wild swimming; a healthy breakfast with like minded uplifting peers.

If you need to, mark out the time in your calendar and make it part of your routine. If, like me, routine is utterly uninspiring, find a way that works for you to make it a daily practice. It might be as simple as setting a reminder, creating something visual that motivates you or leaving little prompts around the house or office.

Part of creating optimum conditions for inspiration and vitality to flow is about removing those things that get in the way and we'll explore that a little later on.

Begin today, in this moment. What is inspiring you and what will you do tomorrow to keep this daily practice going?

YOUR ENVIRONMENT MATTERS

harnessing the power of vital spaces

Have you ever noticed how you feel in different places? Your kitchen probably feels different to your sitting room. A busy shopping centre feels different from a walk in the woods. Your office will feel different to the local pub...well, for most of us anyway.

Your environment has a profound effect on you at many levels. It is constantly sending you signals that you will unconsciously and instinctively respond to and that shape your experience. It affects your memories and the mental resources you have access to. It can alter your language, it can affect your perception of time and sense of future, it can alter your feeling of space and possibility.

In other words, your environment has *power*. As an Empowered Entrepreneur you can harness that power to consciously create the circumstances for your most inspired and creative work.

Your immediate environment has a penetrating effect on your level of vitality. Common sense, and now increasing scientific research, tells us that there are certain environments rich in natural vitality. These include natural places where things are growing, thriving and abundant, particularly forests. It makes sense to spend time there. You can literally plug into that external battery of vital energy and breathe in life enhancing elements.

The Japanese have known this for a long time. Their practice of shinrin-yoku or 'forest bathing' is officially recognised by their National Institute of Public Health as a highly effective means of preventing disease and supplementing treatment. Being in green spaces is soothing, not just because of the colour and relative tranquility, but also because of the terpenes that trees release. These organic compounds, when absorbed through our lungs or skin, have an incredibly beneficial effect on the body.

Spending time in woodland has been shown to reduce anxiety, aggression and fatigue. It is proven to increase mood, improve mental clarity and boost energy and overall vitality. If you are interested in reading some of this research directly then I've included a few references at the end of the book.

CHOOSING WHERE TO SPEND YOUR TIME

Where you do your creative work, where you meet your clients, where you spend your down time, all matter.

Make your workspace a considered choice. Empower yourself to work wherever you need to to get maximum benefit. For example, when I work face to face with clients, a lot of my coaching work is done on a walk. It facilitates better connections, enables greater creativity because of how the brain works when the body is moving, and has the added advantage of exercise and time in nature.

A lot of my other work is conducted via Skype as so many of my clients are located all over the world. I don't work a conventional 8-6, as I fit my work around home educating my children and, with the global time differences, my odd evening hours work really well for me and my clients.

When I need to plan or blast through the emails, I like the buzz of having other people around, so if my husband has the children I'll head to the local coffee shop. If I'm creating a new workshop or working on a meditation, the woods or meadows are the best environment for me to think and germinate ideas. If I'm writing, then the tranquil, light, uncluttered space of my studio office works well.

Spaces that support me in my work

The environment matters not just for you but for your clients, particularly if you meet your clients face to face, host events or give talks or training sessions. When considering the venue for my workshops and retreats I am extremely conscious of the inside and outside spaces. How much light there is, how the room feels, how much physical room there is to move around, how high the ceilings are, the subtle details of what's on the walls, whether I can control the temperature, the space outside the main room and the impression that gives - all these things affect my participants at a conscious and unconscious level and really can make or break the success of an event. I will always favour places that feel spacious with natural daylight and easy access to nature as I know it's where I will get the most benefit for my clients and it will put me at ease and in flow.

'Your environment has power.
Harness that power and consciously create the
conditions for your most inspired and creative work.'

ELIZABETH CAIRNS

BE INTENTIONAL,
CREATE YOUR IDEAL WORK SPACE

It doesn't really matter where you work as much as it matters that you consciously choose it based on how it makes you feel, and the impact it has on your work. Be intentional, empower yourself to create the ideal.

If you do have a more conventional office, shape your space to work for you so that you feel good when you're in it. Ask yourself where you need to be to help you focus. What enables creativity? What qualities does your work space need to have, to remind you that you've got your shit together and you're not just careering from one chaotic event to the next?

What colours make your heart sing? How comfortable is your space and do you enjoy being there? The home office, for so many of the people I've worked with, often doubles up as the guest room/laundry room/dumping-ground-for-all-the-unfinished-stuff-of-life room…if you have to clamber over piles of paperwork, laundry baskets and picture frames to get to work it probably doesn't get you in the best frame of mind for an inspired and productive day. If you don't live near to woodland, bring trees and plants inside to support your wellbeing, you'll still get the benefit of those terpenes. Take control of your environment, make it work for you.

If you could change three things right now about where you work what would they be? How quickly can you make those changes to start enjoying your working environment more?

VITALITY VAMPIRES
and finding your tribe

We humans are a tribal species. We are hard wired to connect. Even if you are more introverted by nature, connection to others is so key to optimal wellbeing that other people will have a huge and immediate effect on your vitality. Certain people will leave you feeling alive, energetic, affirmed, clear-headed and empowered. Others can also drain your energy, kill your enthusiasm, trigger self doubt and leave you feeling, in a word, crap.

Who you spend time with really matters, both at work and outside of it.

As an Empowered Entrepreneur it's important to be aware of this, to give it conscious attention and address those relationships in your life that drain your energy and hinder your growth. Energy spent on the dramas within unhelpful relationships is vital energy that could be better used elsewhere. It diverts attention, inspiration and creative thinking away from your business and gets you in a state that slows down momentum.

Who are the vitality vampires in your life? Whether they have an overwhelming, dramatic effect or something more subtle, it pays to be aware.

Clients of course, can fall into this group, as can friends, relatives, business partners, associates, people in online communities…anyone you spend any time interacting with.

Of course everyone can have an off-day or go through a rough patch. This isn't necessarily about cutting people out of your life. It's about being more thoughtful about when you chose to engage with them. It's about being deliberate about what proportion of your time and energy they consume, and whether the balance makes sense. It's also about recognising that if clients fall into the vitality vampire category you absolutely don't have to take them on. We will dig a little deeper into this in *Getting It Done*.

Running your own business can be a lonely pursuit, even with all the possible connections on social media and even if you have a team to support you. There's something fundamental about honest, open, supportive connection; it both feeds your soul and supports your business. Having the genuine support of someone who believes in you and what you're doing makes all the difference. Having an ally who really understands you and your business to bounce ideas around with, to sound off to when things are tough, to remind you how brilliant you are in those moments when you forget, is the essential companion of a truly Empowered Entrepreneur.

Who are your champions?

Who are those people that lift you up? Who really gets you and accepts you for who you are? Who supports your choices and leaves you feeling better for having spent time with them?

Do you have enough champions who will fly your flag and support your endeavours, who will stretch you and challenge you in good ways, who believe in your potential and encourage you to go for it?

Empowerment doesn't happen in a vacuum, it's a process, and relationships are often at its heart. Taking time to nurture those relationships that you recognise as being true, unconditional and wholly supportive are worth your time and energy. As an Empowered Entrepreneur, your business will be so much stronger for it, and so will you.

ATTENTION

where you put it matters

Where you place your attention will affect your vitality instantly. Not only your physical energy, but also your emotional state, motivation, relationships and your capacity to focus and learn. In fact, the whole quality of your daily experience. As an Empowered Entrepreneur you need to take it in hand and direct it for best results.

Consciously deciding what to pay attention to and how, can be the most emancipating, and empowering thing you can do for your overall vitality, the success of your business and the experience of your life. Whatever is happening in your life and in your work, you can choose where to place your attention.

You can choose to focus on what moves you forwards rather than what holds you back, on opportunities rather than problems and on the present moment rather than fears for the future or regrets in the past.

I'm not talking about glass half full thinking here. This isn't about painting everything in the garden rosy; sometimes things are just awful. There's no getting away from the realities of life. Shit happens. This is not designed to encourage a facade or to feed a tyranny of false positivity. It's about acknowledging what is happening, dealing with it proactively, with the full weight of our emotional and physical resources, and choosing a perspective that liberates and empowers you.

Wasn't it Shakespeare who wrote *'nothing is either good or bad, but thinking makes it so'*? This hints at the power of our mind, and our attention, on the quality of our experience.

Reflecting on your current thought patterns
How do you think at the moment about the difficult or unpleasant aspects of your work? Are they challenges to be overcome? Burdens that weigh you down? Or perhaps to be expected as part of the job?

However your perceive these challenges, whether as slightly inconvenient glitches or major catastrophic events, the amount of attention you give them and the nature of that attention is what will strengthen or sap your vitality.

It's natural to fixate on problems, to be derailed by our emotions when something doesn't go according to plan or when fear and anxiety are triggered by events outside of our control. As an Empowered Entrepreneur your aim is for this fixation to be measured, the unsettling effect of it short lived. When you do face difficulties, quality attention with a problem solving mind is far more effective for your business than constant rumination on anxieties and worries. Deciding to give limited time and energy to those things you cannot change over those things you are able to influence, makes good business sense, especially when you consider it in relation to your vital energy.

Shift your energy in an instant

Think about it. How do you feel in your body when you are focusing on a problem or dwelling on an unhappy customer? When all you see is what's going wrong, where you have that constant internal dialogue of regretful thinking…? How productive are you able to be at work when your mind is occupied by the conversation from the previous day that ended in a row or the worry about an upcoming meeting with a tricky client? Chances are you're not bursting with energy and raring to go. It's heavy, it's hard work, it's draining, it makes you reach for the brownie or the caffeine.

Your state of mind and state of body can be shifted instantly by deliberately placing your attention on something else. It really is that simple. Well, in concept it's simple. In reality I know it's not always that easy. That's OK, it's a skill that takes some practice.

Let's think for a moment about attention as currency, currency you can spend on gaining energy or draining it. Where do you spend most of your mental energy at the moment? What do you find yourself thinking about in your working day, and do some things dominate more than others? Is that what you ideally want to be thinking about? Where would you put your attention if you could?

DEALING WITH CHALLENGES
AND CHANGING THE FRAME

When you have a challenging situation you need to deal with, the lens through which you explore it makes a huge difference.

Don't waste attention currency thinking and talking about all the ways that it's a problem, wallowing in all the unhelpful emotions it provokes, fanning the flames of anger or irritation or resentment. Instead shift your attention to the benefits of the situation and what can be done to solve it. Yes, finding the benefits might take some doing at first, but there will definitely be some, you just need to seek them out.

Changing the frame through which you see the situation is infinitely more empowering. When you're running a business, the more time you waste getting in a state about something, the less energy there is for the work that matters. Solve it quickly, take the lesson and move on. It's the vitality smart option. It's what the empowered you would do.

FOCUSING ATTENTION
WHEN AND WHERE IT MATTERS

As well as a general shift of perspective towards those things that feed your vitality rather than drain it, there is also the everyday business of being able to focus your attention when and where it matters.

Being focused and productive at work isn't always easy, but bring your attention to the present moment and you're more than half way there.

THE FORMULA FOR PAYING ATTENTION IS SIMPLE

Decide to pay attention.

Focus your attention where you want it to be.

Notice when your attention wanders.

Invite your attention back to where you want it.

Simple it is, but it's not always easy. Distractions are common. Attention span is something that requires cultivation; if you haven't used it in a while, like a neglected muscle, it can take practice to gain strength and stamina.

Let's explore that formula a little more deeply.

Decide directs us to the state of mind that originates purpose and action - decisiveness - orientation towards what we want to achieve with commitment.

Focus This requires the reduction or elimination of initial distraction, it uses the senses, particularly the vision, it is an active, alert very present state.

Notice This is perhaps the trickiest part of all. Sometimes we don't even have the presence of mind to realise that we've lost focus, we've just drifted off into something else; a train of thought, social media scrolling…To notice, we must be self-aware, present to ourselves and in our bodies, not just going through the motions. This comes easier to some than others.

Invite is a deliberate choice of words too, it's an invitation to our mind to come back to where we need it to be, not an instruction or a demand. It feels genial, cooperative. It assumes that the mind wants to engage with us in productive and constructive thinking and attention.

Kindness is key

You may notice that the process doesn't come with the added step of *Beat myself up for not maintaining attention in the first place*. This wastes vital energy, creates resistance in the mind to focus and just fills potential creative head space with unhelpful negative self-talk.

Remember, simple as it is, I didn't say it was *easy*. Training the mind is a skill that can, like many others, be mastered over time with practice. But knowing the difference it can make and directing it with more intention, even just 20% of the time, will make dramatic shifts to your experience and the success of your work.

If you are already a meditator, or have tried it in the past, you may well recognise this as similar, if not identical, to the process underlying Vipassana. Meditation, in any form, is the training ground for the art of attention and an essential practice of the Empowered Entrepreneur. This doesn't mean you have to start burning incense, spend hours on the cushion, trade your heels for Birkenstocks and start going on yoga retreats, unless you want to of course… but it does make sense to start utilising one of the most powerful tools in your toolkit. Just like exercise for the body, exercise for the mind is needed so that it's toned and flexible for when you need it most.

GET BACK TO NATURE
where vitality begins

Whoever you are, and whatever you chose to do, forging a strong connection with the natural world is one of the most beneficial things you can do for your own wellbeing and the health of your business.

I believe that being disconnected from nature is fundamentally responsible for much of the malaise and disease affecting our busy Western world and re-connecting to it, the natural antidote to so much of what ails us.

For you to be at optimum vitality, a connection to nature is essential. You can't be all that you can be without it. As we have touched on already, there is so much power to be had, so much vitality, so many benefits to getting literally down to earth.

All those benefits aside, being close to nature reminds us that there is a season for everything, that change is constant. Even when things seem totally barren and dark there is always the potential for new growth. For the Empowered Entrepreneur this perspective is enlightening and enlivening.

Nature asks nothing of you. Just the very fact that you are a living, breathing creature gives you the right to be there, to be part of something greater than yourself. Being part of nature reminds you that everything is indeed connected, that you cannot possibly be alone with all this life around you.

As a creative entrepreneur, the natural world offers you infinite inspiration, shape, colour, texture, movement, light and life in abundance. And when you consider natural environments in relation to your vitality, you have places where you can literally plug yourself into the mains and recharge.

SPACE

the essential component of inspired work

SPACE

the essential component of inspired work

Space is fundamental for every entrepreneur.

Without space your ideas don't have room to breathe, your creativity and flow may be stifled and you can easily become overwhelmed and disheartened.

With no space, you can end up careering madly from one thing to the next, no time to reflect, to assess, to elevate or innovate.

Clarity and space are intimately connected. You need both to make the right decisions for your business and the direction of your work. Clutter, both mental and physical, is the antithesis of inspired businesses the world over. Space isn't always valued in our culture, though, is it? Its place is relegated to beach holidays and weekends in the country, or those obsessed with the minimalism trend. Many people are waiting until their working life is done before they feel they have the right to enjoy a little more space. It doesn't have a position in our working lives that carries the same worth as say, productivity or gross profit. But what if the two were linked? What if, in business, space was a prerequisite for growth and financial success? I believe it is. Space is also often the answer to many challenges faced by creative entrepreneurs, not least overwhelm, lack of inspiration and clouded thinking.

The space afforded by time can also be scary, so we avoid creating it. It's much easier to be absorbed in busy pursuits than risk what might rear its head if we have time on our hands. Busy-ness is comfortable, it allows us to quiet the voices in our heads, to avoid the questions that may require answers if we were forced to hear them.

Never before has the need for space been so prevalent. Our culture and technology has shifted so much that we are losing space. So many things fight for our time and attention that we don't even realise how little space we have until we start creating more of it. Space that enables our ideas to germinate is pushed out. Every free moment is filled with scrolling, updating, liking, absorbing. It's very difficult for the mind to perform two cognitive tasks at the same time, so what we lose is the behind-the-scenes processing from which great ideas are born.

If there is one thing you can do right now that will make a huge difference to your business and your life, it's create to space. Physical space, mental space, emotional space.

This doesn't mean you have to overhaul your entire life, get rid of everything and go all Zen, although if you feel compelled I'm not going to stop you!

This is about stripping away what's not necessary, those things taking up mental and physical energy. This is about being comfortable with the unknown, the unfilled, the creative void and curating your life with intention. To make space is to structure your life in a way that gives your creative process room to breathe, and gives you enough time to deliver your business offerings so that you can do your very best work.

WALNUT

"Everything that grows and
thrives needs space."

ELIZABETH CAIRNS

space

SPACE

The vital aid to your creative process

The creative process isn't linear, it doesn't always happen to pre-defined timescales. To be done well, requires regular access to flow. In the running of an inspired businesses almost every process, particularly the creative ones, will benefit from space.

You need to actively build that space in, during your day, between your projects and in the way you approach your client work. You need to structure your working time in the way that enables you to work at your creative potential and charge accordingly. You need to understand how you work best and buy yourself the time you need to do your best work.

Whilst good for business and essential for creativity, time spent in creative flow is demanding on the body and mind. We use an awful lot of brain energy, and physiological resources like mineral reserves to get into this highly tuned peak state of performance. So you also need to allow yourself appropriate space to recover from bursts of intense, inspired and creative activity that being regularly in-flow requires.

THE PROCESS OF CREATING NEW WORK

When you are creating something new, especially if it's a big project, it rarely all comes together in one sitting, does it? There are points in the process where the flow abates and you need to step away, perhaps to recharge, perhaps to process and think, or to gather information.

This is particularly true for me in my writing process. When I am writing for a client, the whole process takes much longer than the time it takes to actually sit and write the final piece. First I need to understand the scope of the whole project, what's most important.

Then I need to establish the right voice, which means getting right under the skin of my client, absorbing their turns of phrase, their perspective, their values and creating a thesaurus of words to draw from.

I may need to do a period of intense research, loading my conscious and unconscious reserves with information so that I have it at my fingertips when I'm in that place of inspired flow later in the process. I need to get a sense of where I'm heading with the piece, so take time to clarify the outcomes and play around with phrasing and key messages. I might fiddle about with a few sentences in draft format.

Then I actually write it. The writing of it usually happens in one seamless flowing piece, if I've given the process enough space, that is. In between each stage I step away, actively create headspace, absorb myself in something else and allow the themes and words to form behind the curtain of my conscious mind before they are ready to come out and take centre stage.

Without the space, it can be hard to find flow in the writing, the words are forced and difficult, they don't seem to have any magic to them, so they don't sing from the page and really speak to the heart of the reader, which is exactly what you want from compelling copy.

White chestnut: a natural aid
to calm the mind

In the writing of this book, I adopted the same process. The space between active stages was much, much longer in the early days, when I was deciding on themes and testing concepts, absorbing a lot of information from clients and reflecting on my past experience. I could go a few weeks without actively working on the writing.

In the final days of completing the manuscript, in the holidays when I had my husband home to be with the children, the process was condensed. I would write intensely for 45 minutes or up to an hour then create the headspace; get up, rehydrate, hang the washing, walk down the lane, play with the children, and let my thoughts fall back behind the curtain for 15 minutes or so. I would then sit back down and invite them and the flow to come back out again.

I did this for whole days, all the space I'd previously created, making it easy to find the right words again and again. I would work most intensely on the manuscript in the mornings when it was easier to find my flow and use the late afternoons for admin. I built in space knowing that it vastly accelerated the process and produced, hopefully, a better quality of work.

How do you work best? What room do you need to process? What accelerates things for you?

In your business, you need to allow for the space that your own unique creative process demands. It's not something that can be hurried if you want to do your best work.

The scale of your projects, the intricacies of your approach, and how easy you find it to get into flow will all determine how much space you need. Being able to charge enough and manage expectations to allow for that time is key. Educating your clients about your process and finding ways to show the value of what you do will all help with that.

It's worth taking the time to map out and refine your creative process. Where would you benefit from more space and how might you begin to build that in?

CURATED SPACE
the difference between clutter and conscious curation

There are a few curses creatives tend to suffer from the world over, one of which is undoubtedly clutter. It's not a major factor for every creative entrepreneur, but if you have a clutter challenge it will likely be hampering you in a *big* way. If you're going to take control of your business and start owning that hallmark of the Empowered Entrepreneur, it's something you'll need to get to grips with sooner rather than later.

You'll know straight away if it's something you need to tackle because it will be obvious. It will be showing up all over the place.

In your physical spaces; your desk, your office, your home, your car, your wardrobe. In your virtual spaces too: your inbox, your calendar, your social media accounts.

Clutter sends you the message that you don't have your act together. It distracts you from what's important. It overwhelms you and can make you feel anxious, helpless and out of control. Some people aren't even aware of the extent to which it is affecting them until they are free of it.

When you are free from clutter, feelings of calm, tranquility, a sense of peace, clarity and time are much more likely to be a regular part of life.

If you need more convincing that clutter is a problem, there's a mounting body of research that tells us how clutter makes it difficult for us to navigate through our world and get done what we need to get done.

For now, you can trust me when I say the amount of clutter you have affects so much of your experience, not least your ability to filter out irrelevant information and get into creative flow. It affects your ability to think clearly, impacts short term memory, affects your ability to effectively read facial expressions and process other visual information. It contributes to feelings of low self control, indeed, some research has even shown that clutter can lead to comfort eating! Clutter undoubtedly compromises our overall sense of satisfaction with life.

You probably wouldn't send out a client proposal that was cluttered with information thrown on the page any old way. If you wanted it to have impact you'd arrange it, you'd curate down the copy to only what was necessary to make your point in a compelling way. You owe it to your business and to yourself to arrange and curate your space so that it inspires you and supports you. Once you've addressed the clutter curse you won't look back. It will feel so liberating you'll wonder why you didn't just get on and do it before. After all, it really doesn't take much, just the commitment to do it and allocating the time in your diary.

Now I'm not suggesting that you strip everything back, completely clear the decks and sterilise everything. You may be a collector, someone who likes a lot of things around them, tokens of significance, treasures from special places, art, books, music. You may find that you work best with plenty of visual stimulation on the walls, mood boards, clipboards, fabric swatches, quotes, etc, and that's OK.

I'm not suggesting you get rid of all that. A carefully curated collection can be a thing of beauty and an inspiration.

Clutter is not curated, it's something different. It has no purpose, it's mess, it's disorder, it's jumble. It's what happens when you don't give thought to your space or are in too much of a hurry to find a place for things. Clutter is the odds and sods lying about, things that need to be fixed, filed, recycled or simply thrown away. The nik-naks that you don't really love but haven't got round to moving on, or just the everyday items that don't have a home. It's the way things are arranged, or rather, not.

BECOME THE CURATOR OF YOUR PHYSICAL SPACE

Give your mind and your business the best possible head start and only fill it with what is useful and beautiful. If you know the clutter curse has taken hold and need to take steps to get back in control, then your office is a great place to start. Book the time in your diary *now* to clear the clutter in your office and curate your space. Don't faff about, just book in the time. Enlist the help of a friend to keep you on track if you need to, but just get it done. Bit by bit you can tackle the other spaces, you just need to make it a priority and start.

When it's time to tackle it and create some space:

Sit at your desk and take a good look around you. For everything you can see ask yourself, what purpose it this serving? Is it beautiful, inspiring, motivating? It is useful, do you need it to hand? It will be easy to see what is taking up unnecessary space in your office if you take a few moments to really look. You can quickly establish what is clutter and what is serving a purpose.

This simple process, done in small steps throughout your home, will enable you to create a truly inspiring and empowering environment in which to work and live.

HEAD SPACE
the road to clarity and peace of mind

Clarity and peace of mind. I don't think I've met an entrepreneur who doesn't crave those things or recognise how important they are and yet they remain so elusive, sometimes, don't they? It's so easy to feel overwhelmed and lose focus or struggle for ideas and confidence of direction. That's not surprising when there is so much in our heads getting in the way. But there is a path to that clarity and peace that so many of us seek. Head space.

Head space gives you clarity of mind, a sense of order and a feeling of expansion and possibility, and is the opposite of mental clutter. Mental clutter is noise, the accumulation of excess information that hasn't been properly processed or filtered out. It's noise that drowns out the voice of wisdom inside you. It's the unhelpful or limiting internal chatter that serves no purpose and drags you down. It's the constant stream of input from the media that gets taken in and left to fester.

Mental clutter clogs the system and causes you to stagnate, it overwhelms, makes it difficult to filter information and disguises what's important. A prime collection spot for mental clutter is social media. You cannot fill an already full cup. For new ideas to come in, there needs to be space for them, room that isn't being taken up by other stuff, particularly other people's ideas.

When you have head space however, so much more is made available. You are open not only to a flow of ideas, new projects and diverse experiences, but your ideas also have room to establish roots and grow. Innovation is made possible when you have the space to see things in new ways, your wellbeing is supported by more nourishing self-talk and your priorities are set by you, not at the whim of the media or someone else's agenda.

For optimum vitality, synergy and creativity, you need a healthy dose of space from mental input every day. Time when you aren't on social media, reading, talking to someone else, listening to a podcast or surfing the web. It's time to be, time to play. It's the kind of space we probably had more of as children, particularly if, like me, you were born before the digital age, when our parents told us it was OK to be bored and that we should go create our own fun!

91

Creating this kind of head space is actually very easy, you just need to prioritise time for it. The brain processes really well when the body is moving, so activities that don't require you to think too much about them, but stretch and move the body are ideal. A daily run, walk, yoga class, painting a wall, tending a garden, perhaps playing an instrument if you're proficient, that sort of thing. A physical activity you can become absorbed in to allow you time to be alone with your own mind. Even housework counts, which is great news if you've got clutter to clear from your physical space.

The amount of space you need will depend on how fast information flows to you, how much you absorb, how quickly you output your creative ideas, and how much energy you have. But we all need it and more than we are currently getting.

Consider taking extended and regular breaks from social media as part of your usual routine too. If you use it as a marketing tool for your business, take a weekly social media retreat from Thursday night to Monday morning; your creative mind will thank you, I promise. If you can't manage it once a week then once a month will still have you reaping benefits.

As an Empowered Entrepreneur you need to be steering your own ship, which means you get to decide who is at the helm of your thoughts and when you want to be sailing. Turning notifications off on your phone or laptop, then setting a specific time to check messages and emails is one positive step in this direction.

CREATE SOME HEAD SPACE

Get hedonistic with your head space, sprinkle it liberally through your day and just watch your productivity sky rocket. Having a head space hit list pinned on your wall to remind you of all the ways you can create that space can be really helpful. Take five minutes to jot down 10 uplifting ways you can create headspace for yourself. Here's a few of mine to get you started.

Take a dance break Crank up your favourite tune, and let yourself go.

Get into the garden feet in the soil and hands in the earth.

Grab a journal your paints and a pen and head to the woods for half an hour nature journalling.

Take your camera and head round your house, what little vignettes of home life can you capture for posterity?

Light a candle hit the cushion for a spot of meditation. As little as five minutes is enough to get some head space.

FREE-WRITING
a quick route to clear mental chatter

Free writing is an effective process for clearing mental chatter
and calming the monkey mind. I often use it to begin my
working day, especially if it's a busy period. When there's a
lot of information swimming about in my head and getting in
the way of me being productive, it really helps with focus. It
works like this: take your journal or piece of paper and a pen,
set a timer, start at 5 minutes, put your pen on the paper and
start writing. Completely uncensored, continuous writing,
whatever comes to mind and don't stop until the timer goes
off. Don't stop, don't edit, don't censor, just keep writing.
That's it. If you find there's more to write after five minutes
just keep going until you come to a natural end. I find 8
minutes is a sweet spot for a morning routine but you can
play around and find what works for you. I find the practice
so cathartic, with so many benefits, and it's so simple.

Olive: Supports you with
rest and regeneration

CREATING SPACE TO DO YOUR BEST WORK

When you've got a to do list as long as your arm the task of carving out yet more time can seem like a daunting prospect but once you know how much you'll gain it becomes a no-brainer to slow down the pace a little and invite a little more space.

Creating more space makes you not only more efficient, it increases your enjoyment of life and work as you move through it. Rather than careering from one commitment to another, cramming every moment full, with space between things you have time to savour.

In your work, space between tasks and topics enables you to do things well, to pay more attention to detail and give greater freedom to your creativity. Taking time after a meeting to process, to plan, to take the learning and take any immediate necessary action will help you avoid the overwhelm that comes from stacking meetings back to back. It also ensures that valuable meeting time isn't wasted by being muddled by what comes after.

Creating space gives you more of a feeling of being in control, which is priceless. You are less likely to make reactive costly decisions or experience repeated overwhelm, and more likely to enjoy sustained energy and productivity which ultimately reflects on your bottom line.

Building longer blocks of space into your yearly calendar gives you the opportunity to take a wider perspective and work on your business in a way that allows you to elevate your offering too.

SPACE TO ELEVATE

Building in space to plan, to see the wood from the trees and to refocus several times a year in your business is essential. It can renew enthusiasm for your work, spark new ideas, enable you to re-prioritise, help elevate your offering, gain perspective and above all, maintain confidence that you are steering your ship in the direction of your dreams.

This kind of space and reorientation isn't achieved in an hour away from the desk, a monthly review or even a holiday. I'm talking about carving out a chunk of time, a couple of days at least, from your schedule two or three times a year to focus on your business rather than being in it. Time to notice what's working, and what's not and get re-inspired.

Where you spend this time makes a difference too. Getting out of your usual routine, turning off the distractions, including email and social media, and immersing yourself in a new, natural and refreshing environment will greatly enhance the benefits of time away. Remember the power of that nature connection? Make it an essential element of this process and reap all those added perks.

Create space with the seasons and when it makes the most sense
In my business these times happen in spring and late autumn, early winter.

Spring is a great time for me to plan, to conceive of new projects and possibilities, whilst autumn is more reflective, a time to assess what's gone well, what I need to do more of in the following year and what I need to get rid of to create space for the next burst of spring creativity.

It's also important to dedicate time to celebrate, to pay attention to your successes and mark them in a way that is meaningful. Treasuring these times can really help see you through the tough patches. Find a way to thank those who have supported you and thank yourself for all the graft you've put in along the way. Planning a party might not be everyone's cup of tea but if it's yours, why not get it in the calendar and make it a regular feature of your business year?

When does it make sense for you to allocate time to work on your business? Does Spring and Autumn sound right or is there another time of year that draws you? Perhaps the New Year works for you or the summer break when work might be less busy. There is no right or wrong. Choosing the time, protecting it, and making it a regular event in your year is what's important. Mark it out in your diary now so you can plan to make the most of it.

SPACE IN THE EVERY DAY

Simple ways to create more space:

Start as you mean to go on

The feeling of spaciousness can be created at the beginning of your day with a few moments on waking before you do anything else. Check in with how you feel, take a few mindful breaths. Set your intention for the day and start as you mean to go on.

Transition time

Allow yourself time to transition between the phases of your working day and between work and other commitments. If you've got the girls over for lunch for example, don't just get up from the laptop when the doorbell rings. Set a timer so you can leave your work unhurried and set for your next session. Take the time you need to tidy up, set the table, enjoy baking that bread or making that batch of cakes and to clear your mind. You'll find you won't be pulled back into thoughts of work and can make the most of those delightful features of your day.

Set your working hours in advance

Decide which days of the week you want to work and what hours in those days too. It can be all too easy when you run your own business to let the volume of work dictate when you are done. The to do list is never really complete, so set a boundary with your time and respect it. When is it time to stop? It might be different on different days of the week and that's fine too, flexibility is one of the joys of being your own boss after all. It's better to be highly productive for short periods than simply busy all day.

Planning in an enjoyable activity at the end of the working session can help you honour that time too. If you manage a team, set the precedent and decide the culture the want to create. Cocktails or mocktails with them after work could be great motivation to down tools.

Mark out physical zones for different activities

Knowing where activities take place and only doing them in those places can help prevent the bleed of work into other areas of life, especially if you work from home and at home. It doesn't mean you can't take your desk outside or work on the move if that works for you, but it can help keep the boundaries clear if you find them hard to manage.

Dedicate a space for admin or desk specific activities. Create zones specifically for rest or reflection that are screen free. Ban the phone, the laptop and the TV from the bedroom and create a sleep haven. Use outside space regularly and deliberately to invite fresh air and fresh thinking and raise your energy.

Crossing the threshold from one room to another, or one working space to a different one, helps with those transitions and the feeling of space created by knowing you don't have to be at work and working all the time.

Look ahead

Make it a regular practice to review your diary for the coming days, weeks and months and check your social commitments, not just your work ones. Regularly looking ahead will allow you to spot well in advance where you have overloaded and give you the opportunity to redress the balance in good time.

Pause for thought

Pause at the end of a working day to reflect on what worked well, what you've learnt and what comes next. Jot down a quick priorities list which will help you start with momentum and purpose at your next session.

Just three breaths

It's amazing how much space just one breath can create. Make it three; one to calm the body, one to collect the mind, and one to set an intention and you have a perfect spacious moment. Repeat every hour on the hour and that's a whole lot of space in your working day.

Time for tea

Whether you're a tea lover or a coffee connoisseur there's no need to slurp and run or drink at your desk. Making your tea break a break will build in regular space to your day. Opt to take your beverage of choice somewhere different away from your desk. Slow down and pay attention while you're making it and then sit and savour it for the 10 minutes it takes to drink. No phone, no laptop, just tea. Cake is allowed too, of course.

Schedule it in and make yourself accountable

If you know you have a tendency to cram your days full or let work run on into breaks, book yourself in for an activity that forces you to get out of your workplace and doing something else. A post lunch walk with a neighbour who won't cancel on you. A lunch with an uplifting friend. Breakfast with a like-minded colleague. If it's a class, paying for it in advance might help with motivation to honour the commitment.

When you wash the rice, wash the rice

This traditional Zen saying holds the key to that feeling of space and absorption so synonymous with being in flow. Be fully present with what you are doing, while you are doing it, until it's time for the next thing. Then be fully present with that. No multi-tasking, no ruminating or fretting about what you should have done or what you've got left to do, just full engagement in your chosen activity of the moment. It is perhaps the simplest way to create space in everything you do.

THE WORK

shaping an inspired business

THE WORK

shaping an inspired business

As you've no doubt already noticed, I'm a firm believer that working hard doesn't have to feel like hard work and you don't have to wait until the working day is over to enjoy life.

Shaping a successful, self sustaining business is relatively simple. All it requires is a passion to do the work you are uniquely placed to do, a healthy dose of self awareness, and a liberal sprinkling of commercial sense.

As an Empowered Entrepreneur you're not just going to create any old business or do any old work. You are going to do inspired, authentic work at the heart of a well thought through, profitable business, which in turn supports a purposeful and meaningful life.

When you are doing the right work, business is more pull than push, more flow than force, more delight than drudgery. Don't get me wrong, there's no shortage of hard graft, but the energy behind it feels good. It reminds me of a story that my friend Fiona told me recently. Her little daughter Poppy asked her why she had to work, why she had to be a brand stylist? Fi replied so beautifully "you know that feeling, Poppy when it's time to go to bed and you just *have* to finish that drawing? It's like that for me. I just *have* to design brands, I love it so much!"

That hints at the kind of energy that being inspired by the right work can create. It's not something you do grudgingly, you're compelled, and, most importantly, it feels good!

WORK LIFE BALANCE
making it unnecessary

Before we get on with defining the work and refining your inspired business, let's take a look at this concept of work-life balance.

The work-life balance movement has evolved, understandably, out of a need to address the work ethic that has sadly become the norm. That almost universal acceptance, that work should be hard, toil and labour. A utilitarian means to an end, rather than fulfilling in and of itself. That work, or rather the pursuit of money, should be the priority because it's money that supposedly facilitates everything else.

The notion of work-life balance is intended to get you out of this cage, where you feel imprisoned by your job, or the need to earn money and are free to enjoy your time.

There is a suggestion though, in this well meaning movement, that we should not be misled by. It's the suggestion that work and life are separate things. The implication in its very name is that, when you are working, you're not really living, and that has the potential to be wholly disempowering, not to mention thoroughly depressing.

The word balance also evokes this sense of weighing scales that are, ideally, equally weighted. This is problematic. It implies that we need to be constantly managing the scales to offset each period of effort at work with an equal and opposite period of relaxation or time out. It's just not realistic, and flow doesn't work like that either. We need a model that allows for those times when inspiration strikes and we are carried on a wave of creativity too. Without feeling guilty that we aren't quite getting the balance right.

If you're currently taking the traditional hard-labour route to work, it may well feel like not much of a life when you're there, but all that can change. As we discovered in the previous chapter, there are more elegant ways to approach the need for space.

'Working hard doesn't have to feel
like hard work'

ELIZABETH CAIRNS

By taking a more empowered approach to your whole life, which of course includes how you run your business, the need for a work/life balance becomes redundant.

Shifting to a more empowered way of working

The start of the shift to a more empowered way of working is to recognise that you can enjoy your work and earn good money at it. It actually makes it much more probable. It's also to understand that, in many cases, the money is unlikely to be the true end goal, not when you look at things clearly.

I was exploring this concept with a client a while ago. He ran several successful ventures, and was very clear that he wanted to make £300k profit in the coming year from one of them. When we explored what he wanted that money for, it was to put in place the exit strategy from a couple of his other commercial projects. He wanted to free up more time to spend with his family and take a break, as he had suffered a recent break down. When we drilled more deeply into what he would gain from spending more time with his family and taking a break, it was a revelation to him what he actually wanted from his life.

It was to have time to enjoy the simple things. He wanted to luxuriate over dinner with his family rather than always rushing back to the office, to take longer walks with the dog and enjoy the passing seasons around his country home. He longed to be able to do more with a charity project he had a little hand in. When I asked him what those things would enable him to feel and experience he spoke of peace, joy and laughter and meaningful contribution, memories that he could treasure and in particular, of having no regrets.

There are amazing opportunities that can be fulfilled with your work. You can push the boundaries of your potential, achieve truly incredible things. If you feel the call to do that, I urge you to go for it, whole-heartedly and with gusto. The boundaries to push while you do it, aren't necessarily those of your physical or emotional endurance though.

Life is too short to wait

Know that you can do it in a way that feels good in the doing. The cost doesn't need to be paid in your wellbeing or time with your family for example. It's too high a price to pay.

If you long to enjoy the simple things, to take pleasure every day and to find genuine joy in what you do for a living, you don't need to wait. For a happy and meaningful life, it's essential that you don't. It doesn't need to be at the cost of your success. I would go so far as to say it's an essential component of it.

Let's skip straight to that part, and craft a business that is enjoyable in its own right. One run by a sustainable form of energy that prioritises your wellbeing, doesn't deplete you, and forms part of the bigger picture of a life worth living.

SUCCESS
what does it look like to you?

There are countless versions of success. It's something that many are chasing, often without really stopping to consider what it means to them. As an Empowered Entrepreneur, you get to define what it means to you.

Establishing your criteria for success is absolutely critical. It determines the scale of your business, the direction of your work, your everyday choices and where you put your focus.

There are so many models of success out there, many of them thrust at you daily in subtle and not so subtle ways. You can't help but be conditioned by them. If you haven't taken the time to clearly define your version, the chances are you're absorbing other peoples' projections of success and living them out as if they are your own. This can lead to a boat load of frustration, dissatisfaction and rainbow chasing that ultimately ends in an unfulfilled life.

Taking time to consider deeply, to take both the wide and the detail view and to clearly define what success means to you, gives a greater sense of purpose, clarity, momentum and fulfilment in your work.

Success can be an uncomfortable word for some, associated with money grabbing, fame chasing, or vacuous pursuits that feel lacking in substance. Or it can be wholly empowering, conjuring visions of worth, value and abundance. Know that this word can be redefined in any way that has meaning for you.

DEFINE YOUR CRITERIA FOR SUCCESS

Grab a pen and your journal and take yourself off somewhere
beautiful where you have time and space to dig deep and ponder:

What does success mean to you? Jot down your uncensored thoughts.

How do you know you are successful? The reflex is often to think of
work goals and aspirations and this is great. But I would encourage
you to expand your perspective. To think long term and to reflect
more deeply.

What does a successful life look like and what will matter to you at
the end of it?

What is the legacy you want to leave? How are you shaping the
world and how would you be living if you could?

'Let the space between where you are and
where you want to be, inspire you'

INSPIRED BY TRACEE ELLIS ROSS

MAKE A DIFFERENCE

get a mission that matters

Great brands change the world. Behind great brands are brilliant people who have clarity of mission. You may not yet see yourself as a change-maker, a leader, someone of influence but actually we all are. Every day we impact those around us.

The quality of your work, your attitude, how you show up time and time again to do what you do has power to shape and change things. Whether you take advantage of that is up to you. When you work for yourself you have an opportunity.

As an Empowered Entrepreneur you recognise that consciously creating a business that shapes your world is totally within your power. Whether you touch the lives of a few individuals within a local tribe or thousands in a global community, the choice is yours.

What is the change you want to make?

It doesn't have to be earth-shattering, epic or history-making. Small is beautiful too. Wasn't it Mother Teresa who reminded us that we don't always need to do great things but we can do small things with great love?

The key to making that difference is commitment. Recognising that when you decide to make a difference you are committing an act of service, however humble. That commitment totally changes the game.

STAND FOR SOMETHING

When you know what you stand for in your business and what you stand against, so much more clarity is available to you. It supports decision making, clarifies messaging, drives motivation and sends a clear homing beacon to your potential tribe.

One of the things chef, photographer and health coach Nathalie Aubry stands for is simplicity. She understands that her audience are often time poor, exhausted and with demanding lives. Her recipes therefore are always delicious and beautifully simple to make.

Where you stand can drive innovation and new offerings in wonderful and profitable ways. Fiona Humberstone, The Brand Stylist stands for a few key things in her work, one of them being building beautiful brands and empowering business owners to do the same. She stands firmly against poor design, badly delivered. Those two things have come together in so many of her offerings, not least her best selling book *How to Style your Brand* and her very popular online course *Design for Go Getters.*

Entrepreneur and social change maker Michael Ledzion stands firmly for doing the right thing. You can see that principle show up throughout his working life, especially when tough decisions have needed to be made. You can hear more from Michael in my conversation with him for the *Empowered Entrepreneur Podcast* series.

What do you stand for?

You may have an instant answer or it may take a little more soul searching. If you're not immediately sure, there will be clues hidden in plain sight. How you conduct your business, where you spend time and effort and what you find you get most passionate about. What moves you to action? What do you find yourself talking about? What delights you about the way other people do things? We can often see what we stand for in others before we acknowledge it in ourselves.

What do you stand against?

This is often easier to answer. It can be quicker to tap into what drives you nuts, as it's often more recognisable when it shows up as anger or frustration. Knowing this will give you clear guidance on what to avoid in your own business. It can also be key when making decisions on who to collaborate with or which brands you endorse and support.

It can powerfully enable you to drive positive change and solve problems with your products or services too. If you want to eliminate something in a proactive way, providing a viable alternative can transform the market. Thank you Natural Deo Co for your work against toxic deodorants and smelly armpits.

Setting up an innovative economic structure to your business to facilitate change can be hugely powerful. Just look at what Tom's shoes are achieving with their one for one model.

Knowing clearly what's important to you and taking a stance will support you in carving out and holding your niche. It will tell you where the boundaries of your work lie and where your focus should be.

I'm not sure who said it but I've always liked the saying *"If you don't stand for something, you'll fall for anything"*. It's probably true.

Whether you state it explicitly and create a manifesto or allow it to quietly inform your work is up to you. But take the time to work out what you stand for in your business. It puts you on firmer ground. It encourages you to galvanise your commitment and opens the doorway to powerful change.

DOING PURPOSEFUL WORK

it's a wholehearted business

Doing purposeful work is one of the great joys of human experience. It feeds our minds, bodies and souls, has an impact on others and leaves a valuable legacy in the world.

However you came to be running your business, whether you started out deliberately or it has evolved over time, you can, at any time, make the decision to start doing do your very best work and live a life of meaning. This isn't about turning any old hobby into a business that makes money; this is about seeking out the work that is uniquely yours and crafting it into a way of living and being in the world that expresses who you are and shapes everything around you.

As an entrepreneur you are free. To create, to innovate, to transform your work and your life, and it is essential that you do so. The world needs people who are alive with possibility, doing what matters and leaving a lasting legacy.

However humble your aspirations or however big your dreams, taking them in hand with deliberate intention, passion and purpose is what they need to come to life.

So many things get in the way of us doing our best work. Often it's time. We are swept along at the relentless pace of life, driven by other peoples' schedules and demands and so rarely take the time to evaluate the nature of our existence. We may have a niggling feeling of dissatisfaction, of things not being quite right. It's easy to ignore, easy to settle. 'One day I'll get to grips with it all', you tell yourself, 'one day I'll have the time do what I love. One day I'll write that book, take more photos, launch that brand, but for now I need to pay the bills, keep the plates spinning, maintain the status quo...'

After all, rocking the boat isn't comfortable. You won't be able to keep all those plates in the air once the water beneath you gets choppy. Growth can be challenging and growing pains are part of the process. Making a shift towards a more authentic way of being in the world and a deeper connection with our own unique purpose involves some risk. It may mean taking a look at some of the things we have built up around ourselves to keep us safe and comfortable, and small. Taking the step towards empowerment can be a vulnerable process. It can, in the long run change everything, but it doesn't need to be catastrophic. Your whole life doesn't have to change and it doesn't have to shift overnight, either. Empowerment throughout the process is important, not just in the end result. You are in control.

This path isn't for everyone, and it's no coincidence you've found your way to these words. Part of you wants to wake up to what's possible. It's not for the faint hearted, quite the reverse. Doing purposeful work and becoming a truly Empowered Entrepreneur is a wholehearted business that really can transform everything, but you don't have to do it all at once. A sincere desire to begin sets you on the path and you can take it at your own pace, one step at a time.

WHAT SHOULD I DO?

Whether you are starting a new business or defining the next step for an existing one, there's one question that can really clarify things and answer that question of what you should do.

"What would you do if you knew you couldn't fail?"

If you know the answer to that question, then that's all you really need to get started. Go and do that. Fear of failure is a demon that lurks around us all, but has no sway with you, the Empowered Entrepreneur. Obviously the execution of launching that business or taking that next step will take a little work, but you should spend no longer faffing about over what it is you should be doing and just get on and do it.

For many people though there isn't a resoundingly clear answer. So then we go on a little journey of discovery.

RECOGNISING YOUR WORK
doing what you are best at

How do I know what work to do? I know it sounds a little simplistic but when people ask me this question I usually give two answers, "do what you love, and do what you're really good at."

As a creative with an entrepreneurial mindset the chances are there are many things you love and so many things you could do. You probably have a fairly broad skill set and could turn your hand to most things, but that doesn't necessarily mean that you should.

Some of those talents will fall into the category of your work, and they may be split further into any number of businesses, whereas some, it's important to recognise, will be hobbies or purely creative projects. You need to know what goes where.

If your business isn't making you decent revenue, it's not a business, it's an expensive hobby. That is, of course, fine if you want to do things simply for the love and not the money, just make a conscious choice about them, make sure they sit in the right category in your mind and prioritise them accordingly. Some people want to create a financially profitable business, others are focused on creating a body of work. Some want to earn a little pocket money and pursue creative projects. Whatever you choose, be clear about what you're doing and why you're doing it.

It may be tricky for you to pin down just one thing you want to do. You may have lots of skills and talents that are linked in fundamental ways. The key is to recognise that, in order to be successful, you need to contain those things into offerings that make sense and can operate as a business. For that to be possible you need to know you can hold your own in your chosen niche. You need to be good, *really good*.

I know this sounds like a bit of a no-brainer, of course you're going to do what you're good at, it's highly unlikely you're going to go into business as an accountant if your real talent lies in pottery, but it's amazing how many people go into business with something they are OK at, but not necessarily brilliant. This isn't enough and it can make it hard to really own your spot in the market. To make a business out of it, you need to be more than passable, you need to be great.

There will be something that you know, in your heart of hearts, you can do really well. Something that gives you energy when you are doing it and feeds your soul. Something you find easier than other things, almost second nature. That's not to say you haven't put the work in to learn the skill or practice the art but you can deliver it with ease, where other people might find it really hard. You don't second guess yourself and can be confident that you really know your stuff. This is work you will likely have been building up to for a while, a coming together of natural talents, passions and insight to make a unique offering. This is your work.

How do you know you're brilliant? You'll get that warm fuzzy feeling of a job well done, of pride in your work, of knowing that you totally nailed it! And your clients will tell you. Often. You won't have to ask for testimonials you'll just get them, unsolicited, gushing words of praise. You will get referrals, recommendations and opportunities.

CREATING WORK WITH MEANING

Bring an idea to life

If doing what you love and what you are good at still doesn't quite narrow the niche enough for you then ask yourself where you can make the most difference and what is sparking your imagination right now.

Perhaps you have an idea for something the world needs, something no-one else has seen yet. It doesn't matter how big or small that idea. If it's meaningful to you and you have, or can rally, the skills and support needed to bring it to reality, then go for it. The bigger picture of your entire offering can grow over time from that seed of inspiration.

Let your story inform your work

You may not yet know what it is that you love above everything else or that you can confidently do better than most. The life of your work may well be in its' infancy. For you, and for others seeking even greater meaning in what you do, look to your story.

Everyone has a singular story, defined by your unique experiences and the life you have lived. It shapes everything. For you, the Empowered Entrepreneur, it will shape your work too.

What have you experienced in your life that has defined you?

What trials have you overcome, what opportunities have you relished, what insight have you gained on your way? What is it from those key experiences that matters to you, that you want to pass on? Use this to inform your work.

As an entrepreneur driven to make your own way in the world, you have a unique story to tell, a message to share and a way to make a difference that only you can. Create a way to do that, and your work will have meaning beyond measure.

WHAT WORKS FOR YOU, ONE STEP AT A TIME

Finding your niche begins with you

There is so much business advice out there about how to find your niche in the market and be different from everyone else. One approach to this is to look at what everybody else is doing, discover what they are not doing well, and do that. For me this is back to front.

You could create the next product that fills a gap in the market, you could jump on the latest bandwagon or pyramid scheme, you could respond to demand from your clients when they start asking you for things, but that doesn't always mean you should. It doesn't make for an authentic business. As an Empowered Entrepreneur seeking to create an inspired, successful business you must look to yourself, rather than the market, first.

Your niche is determined, predominantly, by two things - what you love and are really good at, and the people you can make the most difference to.

There will be a niche that only you can own that lies at the intersection between your talents and the people you are uniquely and best placed to work with.

Keep things in perspective

The question of what work you should do can become overwhelming and paralysing because you may have given yourself too big a time frame to work with. We think we have to have our entire life path mapped out and our forever career taken care of. This simply isn't the case and we'll look at that more when we talk later about the evolving nature of inspired work. It's OK to start somewhere that feels right and see where it takes you. If you have a vision, you can trust the process to get you there, one step at a time, doing the next thing as it presents itself.

WHO DO YOU SERVE?

Knowing your audience intimately is absolutely key to a thriving business.

It determines everything from how you position your offering, your brand look and feel and brand voice, to which social media platforms you choose. You need to know who you are talking to and what it is that will move them to invest with you.

Long gone are the days when we define our target market in terms of sweeping archetypes and demographics. You need to understand your audience more deeply, be able to connect with them at a personal level and build a trusted connection.

When seeking clarity around your ideal client it helps to have someone specific in mind. Not necessarily a current or past client but someone you know or have met enough to get a really clear sense of. What this enables is for you to get under their skin, see life from their perspective. Know their needs and wants, their hopes and dreams, their pain and their struggle.

It will help you find just the right turns of phrase to really speak their language. It will guide your choice of images and visual reference points. It will direct you towards the right look and feel for your brand and your communications so that they are enchanting and captivating, inspiring and move people to action.

Finding just the right niche is about who you can make the most difference to and the magic that is created when you work with the right people.

There are people out there that can only really be best served by you, who will be attracted to your uncommon magic, who resonate with your unique experience and perspective and who enable you to come alive in your work. When you know what your unique work is these people are easier to identify.

So many business owners set their parameters for their target customers as wide as possible in fear of missing opportunities. Don't fall into that trap. You need to get really specific. Yes no doubt your product or service could be great for whole swathes of the population but there will be a smaller, perfectly formed cross section of people for whom it will be life changing, amazing, essential, the best darn thing they ever bought. *That's* your target.

SERVE A SMALL TRIBE WELL

You may have a desire to reach a very large market
and that's great. Targeting a large market may,
however, compromise the success of your business
if you aren't able to serve them with ease and flair
and do your best work. You can introduce different
approaches and offerings to widen your reach, but
only when you have the capacity to do so in a way that
doesn't compromise the quality of what you do.

WHAT DOES AN IDEAL CLIENT LOOK LIKE?

Well there are the obvious markers. They both need and want your product or service, they have the money to invest in it, they understand the value, (you can always help them out with this bit with a little education), they pay you on time and what you're worth, they rave about you, refer you and generally sing your praises, and they are a pleasure to work with.

Then there are the magic markers. This is particularly relevant for entrepreneurs offering a service but applies to product based businesses too.

Think of a time when you were doing some amazing work, that was using your skills and talents to best effect, with a client you totally gelled with. They were getting a brilliant service and you really 'got' them. It's likely to be work that was challenging for you, where you were playing at the edge of your comfort zone, not the boring safe kind of work you can do in your sleep.

The process itself is uplifting for you because you're tapping into your unique skills and talents, the process is uplifting for the client because you are perfectly aligned. The work is taken to a whole other level and it creates a magic that extends beyond the boundaries of the working relationship.

What you are creating between you is an energy that is hugely powerful both for your business, and theirs.

As a coach I've experienced this so often with those clients I've really clicked with. There's more that goes on than just the conversation we are having. It's almost like we are super charging their business and magnetising it. Opportunities start opening up, the pace of change is accelerated and things start to take on a life of their own without seemingly doing much at all. Just a connection, with the right person, in the right way.

The energy created during the conversations you have with your clients is important. Magic is harder to create if the connections between you are difficult, if you're holding back, if you don't click, if you're not able to show up as your whole self doing your thing in the way only you can do it.

Look for the magic markers

Does working with this client make you come alive? Does it stretch you beyond your limitations? Does it feel edgy, exciting, challenging? Do you feel like you understand them at a deeper level? Do you find things are accelerated for them or for you when you work with them?

If you are selling a product does this client truly value what you offer, do they pay full price willingly or save in order to invest with you. Does your product enhance their life in a way that really has meaning for them? Do they come back time and again and bring their friends with them? Do they really get the ethos of your brand and the message behind it? Is it more than just a transaction for them?

Doing your work with the right kind of people reinforces just how brilliant you are at what you do, it builds your confidence, provides motivation and adds energy to your business that can be hard to create otherwise.

Working with clients that meet both the usual and the magic markers is the ideal and, once you've worked with a few of them, you won't want to work with anyone else.

WHAT'S IT WORTH?

finding the value in what you do

Your work is hugely valuable and so are you. Understanding that, and making decisions for your business on that basis is essential.

It's also essential that you add real value to your clients. You need to know the value of what you do for them and be able to communicate that effectively. You need to feel valued, by your customers, those who support you and, of course, yourself.

It really helps when that sense of value feeds into your self worth, because when you don't have that it can erode your confidence, affect your motivation and throw off your judgement.

You need to be able to innovate around value, finding new ways to delight and add meaning and substance to what you do.

At the very deepest level, when your work is valued by yourself and others, it enables you to reach for more. It gives you courage to go beyond what you might have thought possible. It elevates what you do from a day job to something all together more meaningful.

Value, as you know, isn't just about what you charge, it's also about the experience you create and the change that you make. When you have to put a price on what you do, it's often really telling about your view of your own value. It can bring up some less than comfortable feelings around your brand, your positioning and your worth.

'Other people will find it much easier to
see your value once you do'

ELIZABETH CAIRNS

OWNING YOUR WORTH

Let's explore the mindset that accompanies a robust sense of worth and how you can portray the benefits of what you do within your brand messaging. As a successful entrepreneur I believe you need both. A good grip on the financials and your head in the game so you don't sell yourself short.

It's not always easy to know what to charge and it can be a challenging road to get to the place where you are comfortable about asking for decent money for what you do. But what I do know is this: once you are confident about what you are charging, that confidence extends to your clients.

If you are able to congruently and confidently state your price without internal conflict, you are almost guaranteed to get very little external resistance. In fact it can feel good to both parties. You know you're getting a fair price for your expertise and your clients know they are investing in something valuable which is, in fact, an investment in themselves.

So how do we get to that point? How do you discover your own worth and own it? Thankfully there are many paths to that end destination and they are all enjoyable to wander down.

GAINING A TRUE SENSE OF YOUR WORTH

You could start with any or all of the following:

Ask people whose opinion you trust, what they value about you. Ideally it would be people you know aren't just going to blow smoke up your backside to impress you, as it needs to be genuine to have the desired impact.

Notice and write down what you do on a daily and weekly basis that has a *positive impact on those around you* including but not exclusively your clients. This starts to set your Reticular Activating System (RAS), a particularly clever bit of your brain, to notice your value wherever it arises.

Establish your criteria for worthwhile and valuable How do you know someone or something is valuable to you? Is it because you spend money on it/them, spend time, energy? Is it to do with how it/they make you feel? Whatever your criteria start to get a good sense of it.

Start to pay attention to the *time, money and energy* you spend on your best clients and your most valued friends and relatives. Ask yourself "What is it that I am able to do for them?" And also "what's important about that? "

Self worth and value often requires a *paradigm shift* that can happen in less than obvious ways. Consider taking some time to ponder what value a new born child has.

BEING OF VALUE

increasing the worth of your offering

A rose called by any other name is still a rose. **What you call yourself matters,** it subtly shapes your perceived value. It took me a long time to confidently call myself a writer. To own it, to allow it to shape my experience of my business, and to enable me to charge what I'm worth for it.

How you speak about your work and yourself creates an impression with your audience. If you can confidently claim your worth when you speak, it makes all the difference. If you are an artist, then call yourself an artist, a writer, singer, stylist, designer. Own your craft, say it with pride.

Do the work that makes your heart sing and value and worth follow after. Put this at the core of your work and you may be surprised at the shift that occurs. When you give yourself permission to do what you love, in your own way, you allow your gifts to come to the fore. When you use your unique talents to the best of your ability you can't help but add value.

Find creative ways to meet the needs of your customers Innovating around value keeps it fresh for them and exciting for you.

Likewise finding small, simple yet meaningful ways to delight your customers or your audience is one of the benefits of charging what you're worth. Having the cash flow taken care of means you can afford to be generous. *Find genuine ways to show you care.* Give back, pass it on. Spread the love.

Take care of your business brand Having a well executed brand identity that you are proud of can really help you communicate the value of your business.

Take care of your personal brand This is where all the genuine worth of your business starts. Be impeccable with your word, your business practices and what you stand for, whatever that is. A congruent, authentic, consistent and reliable personal brand is priceless.

THE VALUE OF TIME

There is one asset, the most valuable in your business, that is finite. Once it's spent, it's gone. Irreplaceable.

Time is inextricably linked to value and it's a connection so many of us don't pay enough attention to.

Your time is hugely valuable. Once you really know that in your bones it will be transformative for your business and your wider life. Your time is your most valuable asset.

It is not uncommon for entrepreneurs to downplay or even ignore completely the time they spend on working for clients behind the scenes. For so many it's not even noticed, let alone charged for.

There are countless business owners slogging away in endless email conversations, hours of research, meetings that overrun, meetings they shouldn't even be in. So many fall foul of the black hole of social media or even just doing things they simply don't want to do. All this costs time, time that they can't get back.

How do you want to spend your working hours? What is essential to providing your product or service and how can you make sure that the time it takes to deliver that is included in your costs? We will explore this more deeply when we look at creating an Empowered Process in *Getting it Done*.

How you spend you time is how you spend your life. What kind of life do you want? We will get more to the heart of this question next as I invite you to to explore you, the entrepreneur.

'How you spend your time,
is how you spend your life.
What kind of life do you want to live?'

ELIZABETH CAIRNS

YOU, THE ENTREPRENEUR

the heart of a thriving business

YOU, THE ENTREPRENEUR

the heart of a thriving business

At the heart of a creative, inspired and authentic enterprise is you, the entrepreneur. Your talents, your attitude, your dedication is what makes your business what it is.

When you are empowered, the face of your business changes. You can move away from feeling like you need to be all things to all people and move in a more authentic direction, one with your talents and gifts, hopes and dreams at its heart.

As an Empowered Entrepreneur you bring your whole self to your work. You show up when it matters and you are invested in your own development as well as the growth of your business.

Your work isn't just something on the side or a means to an end. It's not something that you settle for just because it happens to fit around the rest of your life. You take more ownership than that. It matters, deeply. It's intimately connected with who you are and what's important to you. It has purpose.

Being empowered is reflected in how you feel, in your perception of your influence and capability and in how resilient you are. There will of course be times when it feels like it's all going to hell in a hand-basket when nothing seems to work out and business is a bit of a slog. Underneath all that, no matter how hopeless things may seem on the surface, you are never helpless. You can trust in your ability to create, to define, to rise again. At your core is the heart of an Empowered Entrepreneur and that changes everything.

In this part of the book we will explore those things that matter to you and how they relate to your work. We delve into the attitudes and mindset of resilient, capable, emancipated business owners so you can try them on for size. We will get right to the heart of what's most important and give that the attention and focus it needs for you to truly thrive.

BE YOURSELF, WHY AUTHENTICITY MATTERS

Authenticity is the ultimate credibility. When you are authentic there is an alignment between who you are at your core, what you think and what you put out into the world. There is honesty, a degree of transparency and a congruence to your actions that engender trust and build genuine relationships.

Running an authentic business is more sustainable than one which is perhaps not as well aligned, and it's definitely more straightforward. It can give you energy rather than depleting it. It feeds your inspiration rather than your fears or insecurities. It grows your confidence and opens up possibilities that might otherwise elude you.

Perhaps my favourite and one of the most eloquent descriptions of authenticity comes to us from storyteller and researcher Brene Brown:

"Authenticity is the daily practice of letting go of who we think we're supposed to be, and embracing who we are."

There are thousands of artists out there, countless stylists, coaches, photographers, teachers, writers, artisans, you name it. When you look at what people do, it may seem like a crowded market place. But when you dig deeper, when you start to connect with the essence of what makes you come alive, what you stand for and the change you seek to make in the world, you see that there is room for us all.

Building your offering around your unique gifts, your passions and your mission sets you naturally apart. There really is no such thing as competition when you are operating from a place of deep authenticity. It's the best marketing strategy in the world.

CERATO

'Authenticity is the ultimate credibility'

ELIZABETH CAIRNS

'Be brave enough to listen
to your heart'

ELIZABETH CAIRNS

START WITH WHAT'S IMPORTANT
why your values matter

We can spend our whole lives being busy. Creating empires, churning out work, but unless it matters to us, really matters to us, and takes into account the bigger picture of what's most important, there's very little point. We just end up with our days filled full instead of living a life fulfilled.

Knowing what's most important, what you value, is absolutely essential for an Empowered Entrepreneur. Your core values as an individual, and the values of your brand, set the parameters of your work and how you live your life.

Knowing what's important is like having an in-built compass and barometer. It tells you which direction to go and whether the conditions are favourable.

When you honour your values, you get a feeling of rightness and harmony. Even if the circumstances are challenging, there's an internal peace and relative comfort from the alignment that living in accordance to your values provides you. When you don't, you feel off kilter, ill at ease and uncomfortable, and not in a good way.

So before you start business planning or goal setting, take a little time to get in touch with what matters to you in your wider life.

Identify what's important

If you were to distill your life into 8 key areas that are important to you, what would they be? Take a moment to jot down those areas now.

It's best not to overthink it and make sure your work is one of them.

Think about all the aspects of your life that matter whether you feel like you are currently doing well in those areas or not. And if it doesn't come up in your initial brain dump then can I suggest that health or wellbeing be one of the 8? I'm always amazed at how often this is last on the list for most people, or doesn't even make the top 8 for some.

I've done this exercise thousands of times over the years and popular categories are things like:

· Spouse / Significant other · Time with family · Work / business / brand · Financial freedom / security · Health and wellbeing · Spiritual connection / development · Connection to friends / social life · Connection to nature · Time with a Pet · Hobbies / interests (this is often specific) · Creativity · Travel and exploration · Learning

There's a free download for the Wheel of Life available on my website if you'd like a template for this exercise.

How are things right now?

Once you have your list, without over-thinking it, give each one a rating on a scale of 1-10 in relation to how well you feel you're doing in that area at the moment. It's subjective, and don't get freaked out by your answers, just instinctively rate each one. This should take moments rather than minutes.

By making yourself aware of what's important and reviewing where you are in each area periodically (every six months works well) you may be surprised at what unfolds. Without needing to do anything else, we begin to naturally prioritise those things we have defined as important.

How does this relate to your work?

You need to understand where your business fits within the bigger picture of your life as a whole and ensure that it supports what's important instead of competing with it. Everything has a place and you can determine what gets priority. It's also about understanding the impact of all areas of your life on your business and recognising that, as an entrepreneur, everything is not in separate neat little boxes; they are all inextricably linked. This helps you shape your business in a way that works holistically. Working holistically is so important as an Empowered Entrepreneur. We need to work with all aspects of ourselves and bring everything into alignment if we are to live the meaningful and successful lives we deserve.

Now you have established the areas of your life that are most important and got a sense of how each one feels at the moment take a moment to consider which ones you wish to make the priority for the next few months or year. Perhaps pick three, for whatever reason, that you would like to focus on improving or dedicating more time to. This will help greatly when making decisions with your business as you can take into account your pre-determined priorities and how to avoid conflict and make everything work well together.

Know how everything fits together

One of the things I notice is that business owners often unwittingly squeeze in lots of areas of their life into the category of their business. The need for a social life or pursuing hobbies and interests, for example. It's fine and fabulous if your business ticks lots of your boxes for you but it's important to recognise that it doesn't always make good business sense. It can lead you to making the wrong decisions for your work because you're being pulled off track by the need to fulfil a value that is being neglected elsewhere in your life. Make the space you need to honour those values that you know in your heart of hearts don't need to be fulfilled solely by work.

You may also find that you can be fulfilling more of your values with your work than you initially thought possible. The desire to travel, for example, doesn't need to be confined to the holidays, you just may not have considered giving it a place within your work. Health and wellbeing is often seen as something outside of the scope of our working life, almost the polar opposite for many. For them, fitness fits into outside of work time and they have to balance the negative impact of their working life and make up for it elsewhere. This is counter productive, doesn't make for a sustainable business and just doesn't make sense. As an Empowered Entrepreneur your business can enhance your wellbeing and in my view, it absolutely should.

Take the time to reflect on everything you've discovered as you've explored what's most important to you at the moment. Notice how everything fits in to place and what, if anything, you might need to change as a result.

THE WHOLE PICTURE
how the pieces fit together

There can be a tendency to look at the different areas of your life as distinct silos. You might work on your 'relationship' or your 'fitness', your 'finances' or your 'hobbies', behaving almost as if they are isolated arenas and disconnected from each other. The separation is most marked, I find, between work and the rest of life.

In the extreme, and as we touched on in the myth of work-life balance, work might be seen as something to get through, a means to an end, something that provides the currency to enjoy things that happen in non-work time. Here is an opportunity for you to step back and take the holistic view, one that encompasses all seemingly discrete aspects of your life experience and recognises their interconnectedness. One that sees the flow between them. In my view, this is vital to the creation of a successful business and a thriving life.

Your business is one cog in a wider system
When you work for yourself it's vital to recognise that your business is just one cog in a much larger system. It can be all too easy to fool yourself into thinking you can look at your businesses in isolation of the other aspects of your life. This simply isn't realistic for an Empowered Entrepreneur.

A business owner finding things difficult or struggling to make ends meet might, sensibly, pay attention to the workings of their business. Checking they have a strong brand that they're proud of, good exposure, a solid reputation, high quality products and services that are both needed and wanted by their target market, these are all key. It's also probably a good idea to engage the right experts to give you the sound advice and support in those areas. Where the creative entrepreneur often falls down, in my view, is that they stop the enquiry there. They rarely look further than the confines of their business.

You can spend so much time looking for the glitch in your business that's getting in the way of ultimate success and fulfilment, not realising that the spanner in the works might be stuck in a totally different cog! When you look at the bigger picture there can be hard choices to make. You can't always have it all at once and you need to decide what matters most. As an Empowered Entrepreneur you don't hide from those choices. You look at the reality of things, challenge your assumptions and move forward with clarity and purpose.

This might mean accepting that it's not the right time to launch your new business, or it might be the wake up you need to get going with things you've been sitting on for too long.

Dealing with challenges in the areas of your life outside of work might get bumped to the bottom of the list of priorities, especially if cash flow is lacking or time is tight. Letting symptoms of dissatisfaction fester will impact your creative work and your business, whether you are conscious of it or not.

The journey of an Empowered Entrepreneur therefore is one of personal authenticity. When you start to operate more holistically, rather than shutting off aspects of yourself or your life that you don't have time to deal with, everything flows better and success naturally follows.

WHEN VALUES LEAD THE WAY
avoiding the resentment of second best

A holistic picture of what's important to you helps define the scale and scope of your business in a way that feels good and doesn't feel like settling for second best.

Having that good grip on your values and which are most important, enables you to be clear about what you are prepared to do and what you aren't. It helps you mark out your boundaries and accept the compromises that come with them. Even the tough decisions are made easier when they're values based and you are prepared for the consequences.

Let me share a simple example from my own life. I have so many dreams and plans for my own businesses. The weekly influx of new ideas for what I could create and new opportunities that I could take advantage of, is mind blowing sometimes. I also like to work fast. I enjoy being productive and the buzz of collaboration of connecting with people and of new experiences.

All of that is true, though what's also true is that I have made a decision to spend a lot of my time, most of the typical working week in fact, with my family, especially while the smalls are still small. Our desire to home educate, our choice to run several creative enterprises rather than just one and my priority to honour my wellbeing and therefore refuse to work myself to the point of burnout, means we have a lot less bandwidth for the quick fulfilment of all those dreams and plans. It could be hugely overwhelming and frustrating, and sometimes it is, but most of the time I'm really OK with it. I'm contented because *I've made the choice*. Deliberately, considerately and in alignment with what's most important to me. Yes, things move a lot slower than they might if I made different choices, but because it's in harmony with what's most important to me, it doesn't feel like settling or second best, it feels *good*. Ask yourself where you want your boundaries to be and understand the consequences. What is most worthy of your time and energy at this point in your life?

SHOWING UP
what it means to be invested

You can spot the entrepreneur who is really invested in their business at fifty paces. There's a different quality about them. They know what needs to be done and they are getting on with it, and not just going through the motions. There's passion, fire, enthusiasm and a work ethic that sets them apart.

They are invested. Playing all in. They have skin in the game - enough riding on it to know they can't just rest on their laurels, that they make a difference, have an impact and are consciously creating something of value.

Showing up for your work, really showing up, being fully present, giving it all you've got and taking the risk to be seen, is hard. There's no getting around it. It will bring up your insecurities, challenge you on so many levels and stretch you mind, body and soul.

You will need to learn new skills, be committed to understanding the workings of a successful business and make changes. You will need to invest in yourself and your own growth. You will need to put yourself out there, be prepared to fail. You will need to do what's uncomfortable...all this and more.

But the rewards are worth it. The connections you will make, how much you will grow, all you will learn and achieve and the possibilities for abundance are immense.

Stepping up comes with a decision. A decision to really take ownership of your business and be the person you need to be to make it successful. Not everyone has what it takes to be a successful entrepreneur, and that's ok, there are many paths to fulfilling work and an empowered and meaningful life. You probably know in your heart of hearts if it's really for you.

Showing up takes commitment. A commitment to step into the fire of the empowered entrepreneur and rise like a phoenix. If I had to choose between going through the motions or going through the fires of transformation, I'd choose the latter every time.

So what's it to be, are you ready to fly?

BEING UNCOMFORTABLE

is highly recommended

Being a successful entrepreneur isn't a comfortable business, quite the opposite, it requires a level of discomfort. Things need to stretch out of shape a bit in order to move beyond the confines of what is staid and safe and create something new and marvellous.

But discomfort isn't the devil, apathy is a far more treacherous foe.

The adversary of apathy pops up every time you get the chance to kick back and take the easy route. To stay on the couch instead of going for a run, to avoid putting your work out there because it makes you feel vulnerable, to avoid challenging a difficult client because it's easier just to shut up and put up.

The Empowered Entrepreneur gets comfortable with being uncomfortable. You know that taking a stand, showing up and stretching yourself is par for the course. But there is wisdom in how you approach it. You don't have to go all gung-ho and throw yourself in at the deep end at every opportunity; that doesn't make for sustainable growth. Rather, to make stretching work for you, it's a gradual, constant process.

Experiential education specialist Karl Rohnke developed his comfort, stretch, panic model as a tool for personal growth and it's one I use time and time again in all areas of my life.

The model is simple. There are three zones:

The Comfort Zone In this zone are all those things that you find easy and comfortable, safe and perhaps even dull. This is the area of sameness and familiarity.

The Stretch Zone This is where things are more out of the ordinary, where there is novelty, growth and adventure. This is the area of learning and challenge.

The Panic Zone This contains everything that currently induces panic because they are a stretch to far. I don't mean mild anxiety, I mean heart racing, mouth drying, sweat causing panic. This is the area of primal fear.

What falls into each zone will be different for every person. For many, public speaking sits firmly in the panic zone, whilst for others it's a walk in the park. The model is dynamic, so what sits in each area can and will change. Your comfort zone can both expand, meaning more in your experience is comfortable for you and you have to grow further in order to find new stretch and challenge. Or the opposite can be true, it can shrink and more and more of life's experiences can become anxiety or fear inducing.

It is a really powerful model for change and development. If there is something you wish you could do that is currently a huge stretch or even panic inducing for you, you can apply this model consciously to bring it into the realms of what's comfortable.

USING STRETCH FOR PERSONAL GROWTH

When we use it as a model for personal growth, we aim to increase the amount of things in our comfort zone by moving regularly out into the stretch zone and back to comfort while avoiding panic all together. Panic is not recommended, It's not an elegant way to approach personal or business development, it floods the system with unpleasant hormones, creates unhelpful associations and frankly, feels pretty horrible. Stretch, however, is great fun. We need challenge for growth, it's what keeps life interesting, engaging and worth living.

Using the model works something like this. Imagine an elastic band represents you and the area inside of the band represents your comfort zone. Imagine taking that elastic band and putting it in the freezer overnight. In the morning you take it out and quickly stretch it as far as you can. What happens to the elastic? It probably breaks. If you want to widen the area inside the band you just stretch it a little, and then let it return to its original proportions, then a little more and relax it back to its comfortable self, then stretch again, a little more and a little more until gradually you have a wider circle. We take the same approach. You do a little of what stretches you every single day, your tolerance builds, the proportions shift and soon enough you're on that stage addressing an audience or in the room with your dream client.

Here's the coolest thing about the model. You don't have to be stretching directly in the direction of the goal, any stretch in any context will still increase your comfort zone all round. The key is to do things that are unfamiliar, challenging, different, exciting, mildly anxiety inducing every single day. They don't all have to be major, even something like wearing your watch on the other wrist changes things up a little. You get to be creative.

What happens if you don't stretch?

For those of you thinking it sounds like a whole load of effort and you're quite happy where you are, here's the rub. If you don't chose to stretch, you can't just sit back on your comfy laurels, because your comfort zone will rapidly start shrinking.

It's similar to what happens to muscles after following an intense prolonged gym routine for a few months then suddenly stopping. After a short while, it's as if you never went to the gym in the first place.

As an Empowered Entrepreneur your stretch zone is the playground of life. 10% stretch every day makes the magic happen. Experiment, challenge yourself, go wild, you never know what you might make possible.

A FEW SIMPLE WAYS YOU CAN PLAY WITH STRETCH

Shift your environment Work somewhere completely different. If you're used to quiet while you work, challenge yourself to write in the middle of a busy coffee shop, train station, supermarket even. Go somewhere unexpected, visit the airport and people watch, hop on a train with no end destination in mind and get off where the mood takes you. Change the orientation of your desk.

Swap something Coffee for tea, right hand for left hand, running for swimming, walking for running, fact for fiction, papers for poetry, pasta for pomegranates, anything goes.

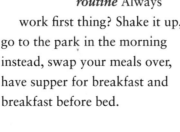

Shake up your wardrobe Wear something different, daring, delightful.

Shift your routine Always work first thing? Shake it up, go to the park in the morning instead, swap your meals over, have supper for breakfast and breakfast before bed.

Speak a different language This really is stretch of the best kind as it gets your brain firing and rewiring in a major way. If you don't know a second language, now's the time, just 10 minutes a day is a great stretch.

OH THE PLACES YOU'LL GO!

When you make the decision to stretch yourself, you are actually deciding to fall in love. To fall in love with learning. Learning new things is the ultimate stretch and in doing so you also honour the fundamental drive of your human nature. You are a learning instrument. You can't help it. From the moment you were born it happened naturally and you have been intrinsically rewarded for it ever since. Learning feels good, it makes things possible and it creates opportunities. As an entrepreneur there is so much to learn and when you empower yourself to take your business in hand you can passionately embrace that opportunity.

This comes with one caveat. You are absolutely not allowed to become the perpetual student who uses learning as another form of procrastination. I've seen it time and time again; the business owner who needs just another course, just another certificate, just another string to their bow before they are ready to begin their work.

Use the opportunity to learn in your work as one to grow your understanding, explore new passions, get to grips with the fundamentals of running a business. There are so many possibilities open to you. To learn is to live.

What have you always wanted to learn? Making the space to do it will feed your soul and feed your work.

MIRROR MIRROR ON THE WALL...
forging an empowered identity

How others see you in business matters. How you see yourself, matters more.

The labels you give yourself, your sense of how much control you have, and what you tell yourself on a daily basis, all shape your feelings of worth and your perception of power.

We all see life through filters and no two peoples' filters are the same. They are determined by your unique history, physiology, environment and behaviour, but they aren't set for life. You can change them, in the same way you might change a pair of sunglasses. As an Empowered Entrepreneur you get to choose the sunglasses with the tint that helps you see the world and yourself in the best possible light.

Exploring your self perception
How would you describe yourself now? With no particular agenda in mind, write a quick uncensored description of yourself, your physical traits and your character, your skills and your drawbacks.

Take a look at what you've written. What kind of picture did you create? What did you focus on? Do you like the person you've described? Do they strike you as an empowered business person?

Now imagine that you can see the best version of yourself, you know, the you that shows up when you're doing your best work and really owning it, when you know you've totally got what it takes. Take a moment to really make that picture vivid. How would you describe *that* person?

Reminding yourself that you are that strong, capable, confident, sometimes funny, maybe even sassy, person and choosing to pay attention to those things *first*, are what help you forge a more empowered identity.

There will always be times when you haven't got it together, when you feel you can't cope, when you wish you looked different or were better at x,y,z but as an Empowered Entrepreneur there's a deep rooted resilience and a clear recognition that you are a force to be reckoned with. So write it in neon and stick it up on the wall, get it tattooed or framed on your desk, do whatever you need to do to remind yourself daily of the amazing and awesome person you *really* are.

STAYING TRUE

maintaining connection to
what's important

STAYING TRUE

maintaining connection to what's important

When there is so much vying for your attention in business, so many competing priorities, so many possible opportunities to pursue, how do you know which way to go? How can you maintain a course that you can trust will end up in the right place whilst ensuring a journey that is joyful and meaningful as it unfolds? The answer to this lies in your ability to tune in to your innate wisdom, to embrace your individuality and stay rooted in your authenticity.

There is so much that might interfere with that connection to your authentic self, that can sow the seeds of doubt or confusion in your mind. The practice of staying true is just that, a practice. It takes a willing heart and a diligent mind to continually work to align how you live and work with what's most important, to act honestly and congruently in everything you do.

Staying true to your mission, your purpose, your unique vision, takes courage and a bit of bloody mindedness. You need to be able to stick to your path, confident in your own choices. You need to be able to cut through the noise and stay in touch with what's important.

Having a way to align with what matters most, to discern the right direction and to stay true to yourself, therefore, is vital. Being able to recognise when something is masquerading as favourable and knowing how to navigate when things get tough, is the focus of this part of our journey as you begin to learn the Art of Discernment.

INSPIRATION IS NOT IMITATION

We all need inspiration and many creatives find that inspiration in the work of others. It's a beautiful thing. You can appreciate the beauty and skill in other people's work and allow it to inform and inspire you.

Staying true to your unique creative work requires that you recognise the distinction between inspiration and imitation.

Inspiration is a unique force that feeds and shapes your business and your work. Imitation is what kills it and can be really damaging to your brand. Your brand has to own your unique spot in the market, your offerings will be born out of your unique skills and vision. Start imitating, in whatever form, and your customers can no longer discern that magic that sets you apart.

I don't believe that anyone creative sets out to directly copy other peoples' work; usually it's a result of an over crowded creative mind and too much focus on external information. Not enough paying attention to your own unique perspective.

What you may not appreciate is all that supposed inspiration and information you are collecting via Pinterest, Instagram etc and the wider world, doesn't function as inspiration without space. Without space it can easily just end up in imitation.

That information needs room to synergise, be woven into the fabric of your own experience and come together as your own. There needs to be time for germination and mental processing that happens beneath the surface.

Without perspective and subconscious synergy, all the richness available to you in that information just covers and smothers your creativity rather than feeding it. It feeds the fear of missing out gremlins and 'I'm not good enough' thinking. You risk creating just another cookie cutter business, following the herd and struggling to keep up.

If you want to innovate, look for inspiration outside of your field, and not just to other arts, look to different environments and cultures. Give yourself space to digest it, for it to come out in its new form, in its own time. Some of the best artists and the most innovative work has been inspired by crossing the boundaries of context and seeing what's there with new eyes.

THE ART OF DISCERNMENT
a process for making authentic choices

Empowered Entrepreneurship is not unconscious, it's intentional. Harnessing intuition, instincts and your mind for success in your business, self determination, creativity and joyful living is how you operate as an Empowered Entrepreneur.

The Art of Discernment is a process that helps you see which choices are the right ones for you, those that align with your values, will move you in the direction of your purpose and are good for business.

Three obstacles to sound decisions for your business
Being driven purely by revenue rather than assessing the true cost or value of a decision.

Being misguided by the **influence of well-meaning others** and not trusting yourself.

Giving too much weight to **what others might think.**

Every decision, even the great ones, will incur a cost. Both if you make them and if you don't. Assessing the viability of an option only on the basis of your bottom line leaves you vulnerable in your business. It often leads to short term thinking, doesn't always honour your values or greater goals and can lead you to compromise on quality. Factor in all costs and value not just the financial ones and play the long game when you need to. Be sure to include the opportunity cost. What opportunities might be lost to you if you don't pursue this option? It's not always about money in the bank in the short term.

Everyone who cares about you, and even those who don't, will have an opinion about how you should run your business. It can be hugely valuable to gain the perspective of others who have gone before. To learn from the mistakes others have made and avoid repeating them. But do so with caution. Making it a habit can start to undermine your own confidence. There is a difference between occasionally taking strategic counsel and unwittingly abdicating ownership of your business by letting someone else call the shots with their advice. When seeking input, consider the credibility of your source. Do they have particular expertise in that area? Do

'Every answer is inside you.'

ELIZABETH CAIRNS

they fully understand the situation? Do they have a vested interest? Do they have your best interests at heart?

Check with yourself why you are seeking their advice in the first place. Is it because you recognise they have experience that you don't or is it because you doubt your own judgement? Ultimately only you can make the decisions that will be right for your business. Only you know, deep down, what is most important to you and what you are capable of. Even if you're not always conscious of it.

Worrying about how you might be percieved can scupper the most brilliant ideas, the most ground breaking opportunities and the most creative of entrepreneurs. When all the noise of the day is done and all those others have gone to bed, it's yourself you come home to. You live with your choices in your own heart and mind. No-one else takes that on.

There comes a point where you get to decide who is driving your bus. Whether fear of looking like an ass is more important to you than going for what matters. Whether back seat drivers get to navigate or you decide which roads make for a better ride. It's a decision you only need to make once and it's done. You'll never need to waste energy on it again. What's it to be? Will you forever let others sit in the driving seat of your business or will you take hold of the wheel and go your own way?

MAKING SAGE CHOICES
don't limit yourself to logic

So many business decisions are traditionally made in the head with pro's and cons assessed and logical options opted for. This is both really useful and potentially limiting. When you need to make a congruent choice between available options you need to be able to use more information than your conscious mind has access to.

Your powers of discernment lie in your physical body, not just your mental process. To use the Art of Discernment you first need to appreciate the wealth of wisdom that your body contains and it's ability to respond to and process so much of what is beyond your conscious capacity.

Your body is taking in information through all of your senses all of the time. You don't need to consciously pay attention, it just gets sorted and processed according to what is most relevant, useful and timely at any given moment. Your body learns, through muscle memory and other faculties, everything you need for optimum performance. Your body has stored all the experiences you have ever had, filed for retrieval when appropriate.

You don't have every-day conscious awareness of this treasure trove of data, but that doesn't mean you don't have access when you ask for it. Just think of how effortless it is to drive a car without thinking, once you get past that incompetent learner driver stage. How easy it is to hold a conversation with a dear friend, just by intuitively knowing how to be with them in a way that is comfortable for you both. How you instinctively know, if you pay attention to it, whether a client or your child is telling you the truth or not. All of these things rely on your body and the power of your unconscious mind to communicate to you in ways that are intelligent, instant and informative, so you can act accordingly.

Your body has valuable information to impart and its capacity as a whole far outstretches that of your conscious rational mind. Deliberately harnessing that power is a daily practice for the Empowered Entrepreneur.

There are three key areas of the body I regularly consult for their distinctive wisdom. My head and associated mind, my heart and related values, my gut and its instincts.

Before we get into the specifics of accessing those resources remember you already have a powerful compass for your direction.

THE ART OF DISCERNMENT

making congruent choices

Use your values as a first filter

Your values and your mission are your first sanity check. Running any decision through the filter of what's most important and where you are ultimately headed, will give you an initial sense of whether it is worth pursuing for your business.

All decisions have their time

Make a decision when it is time for it to be made and not before. So often it is hard to gain clarity over the way forward simply because it isn't the right time. Asking yourself the question 'is this the time for this decision?' will invariably yield a strong sense of whether you are wasting time and energy before it's due.

Sometimes a decision can be the right one, but the thing making it feel wrong is that you have put the wrong timescale around it. Have you made unconscious assumptions about the duration of this choice for your business or your life? Giving yourself permission to do something that feels right now but that may change in the future can give you the momentum you need to take action in the right direction.

Generating options opens possibilities

If we get stuck making a decision it is often because we oscillate between what we perceive as two choices and neither are ideal. Bringing more options to the table and inviting a more flexible mindset, increases the likelihood of finding a solution that is fully viable.

If it's a fully congruent decision it will be easy to make

The more your choice supports and is supported by your core values, mission and purpose, the better it will feel to make. It's easier to summon commitment when it's the right thing for you, even if getting there might seem like more work. I worked with a lovely client recently who was struggling to make decisions about the direction of her company. When we dug a little deeper, she shared a vision for a new venture that just blew me away with how perfect it was for her. It aligned fully with her values, her lifestyle, her creative passions, her skill set and a need in the market. She didn't even have that option on the table before. As soon as it was, she could see clearly why it was so hard to move forward with the other work. It just wasn't right any more.

Assess the real risk

A decision can feel risky even when it's not. If you're struggling to move forward, one way to assess risk is to ask yourself what it would take to return to where you were before you implemented this decision. Most choices we get stuck on everyday involve fairly low risk. Choosing to have children is an exception, it's not so easy to put them back. ;)

With those things in mind if you still have a decision to make and you'd like a surer sense of whether it is favourable you can consult your body.

181

ACCESSING YOUR BODY WISDOM

You can get a general read on whether something will be a good move for you by using what your body already knows based on past experiences.

First you need to calibrate, that is get a physical sense in your body of what a good decision feels like and the opposite.

This is really simple. Think of a time when you made a choice you regret, nothing major just something you know (and probably knew at the time) wasn't a good move. It doesn't have to be in the context of work. Imagine making that decision as if it's happening right now, in this moment, and notice how your body feels. Pay attention to the quality of your breath. Notice any sense of weight or restriction and where that may be. Pay particular attention to your jaw, belly area and chest. Notice if there is any movement in your body. Jot down the key points to help you remember. Now shake it off, literally, move your body to dislodge any resonance of that feeling.

Now think of a time when you made a great choice, for whatever reason, you know it was the right thing. Follow the same process. Imagine you are in that moment, as if it's happening now. Pay attention to how you are breathing, the feeling in your chest, your hips, your feet and your head. Notice if there is any motion in your body, however subtle. Notice the quality of lightness, expansion or sense of freedom, where do you feel it? Jot down the key elements of your experience. Shake it off.

Now hold the decision you currently have to make in your mind and body as if you have already made it. How does your body feel? I'm not talking about emotions which are just labels for feelings, I'm talking about the sensory experience in your body. Does it have the qualities of heaviness, tension and aversion, which are likely to be more like your first calibration? Or more of the qualities of lightness, ease, expansion? Perhaps it's neutral.

In case you're in any doubt, decisions that are in alignment with your values, purpose, passion and body wisdom will always feel lighter and freer than those that aren't.

From this very simple five minute exercise, you will likely have a strong sense of whether your option is worth pursuing. If you'd like a guided audio version of this process, there is one freely available on my website.

If you don't get a clear read, go back and check against the things to remember. Is it the right time? Do you have the right options on the table? Have you assessed and mitigated the risk?

If you still aren't clear it may be that you need a little more information. Your body can help with that too.

ACCESSING HEAD, HEART AND GUT WISDOM

As I mentioned, parts of your body are particularly good at offering you varying perspectives. Logic, reasoning and critique are the domain of the head. Values, social dynamics and higher purpose are the specialty of the heart. Survival, passion and instinct are the realm of the gut.

All these faculties combine to form a greater sense of intuition that can yield you profound insight. You can access any or all of these parts of your body at any time. It can be an effective shortcut or a means of prolonged enquiry as appropriate. I find it particularly helpful to explore a challenge more deeply and give me new avenues to explore. First you need to connect with the relevant area of the body.

Checking in with gut instincts
Let's start with the gut. It's usually the quickest and easiest due to its instinctive nature. Stand or sit comfortably and rub your hands together to generate a little warmth. Place your hands on your lower belly and notice the heat there. Invite your breath down into that area of your body and maybe sway a little with the intention of moving your focus of attention and energy down to your lower body. When you have a strong sense that your energy is rooted in your gut you can begin your enquiry. How do you know you're in the right state? It's unlikely your head will be buzzing with thoughts or you feel spacey and light. It's more likely you will feel grounded, heavier towards the lower half of your body. Your breathing may be slower and lower in your lungs, perhaps more shallow if you are particularly relaxed. You will be aware of your belly underneath your hands more than anything else. It doesn't usually take too long and if you're not sure just try it, it will work anyway if you trust yourself.

Ask your gut a question. You can ask a yes or no of the gut and it will often throw out a quick response. If you've been struggling with a decision for some time though you may need to be a little more clever in how you approach it.

Your conscious mind may get in the way if it assumes that you don't really know the answer. If this is the case ask a question that generates a question. For example: "Gut, what is the question I need to ask myself to move forward in this situation?" Allow the question to sink into the gut and wait until a response arises. The nature of the response will be unique to you. From experience, those from the gut tend to be quicker, more concise and more confident than those from other parts of the body. You may get words, images or feelings or a combination in response. Try not to make judgements. Just notice what it's like for you and make any notes you need to before moving on.

Gaining mental insight

The head is usually where I go next. You follow the same process. Connect with your head in a way that brings you energy up to your brain and top of you body. You can place your hands there or try balancing an orange, even an imaginary one, on the crown of your head. Lift your breathing, make it lighter, lift your eyes and draw all your awareness up to your head. Your head will rarely give you an instinctive yes or no so I tend to skip straight to a more strategic enquiry. Something like "What do I need to consider in relation to this decision?" Or "What question should I ask myself to gain more insight into this decision?" Again, notice the response you get. It may be more rational, logical in a different voice. Perhaps more wordy than the language of the gut. There's no right or wrong, just notice what it's like for you.

Letting your heart speak

Lastly I check in with the heart. The responses from the heart can take a little longer for many people and tend to have a more emotional quality. To connect, plant your feet firmly in an open comfortable stance. Warm your hands and place them over your heart. Breathe deeply, filling and expanding your lungs beneath your hands. Allow your shoulders to relax. Close your eyes if you feel comfortable to. Bring a slight smile to your face. Settle into this comfortable, warm, open space with all your awareness on this part of your body.

Good questions for the heart are "What is most important for me to consider when making this decision?" "Who do I need to pay attention to in this situation?" "What could I do to create more ease and joy in this situation?".

Give yourself the freedom to play and explore. You can try different questions, times of day, body positions, alternative sequences. There is no wrong way to do this. As long as you respect and trust your own innate wisdom, this will prove a hugely powerful tool for unlocking potential and discerning your most authentic path.

It's possible to develop a finely honed feel for the right way forward and the signals of when to hold back or explore other options. With practice, these processes becomes instinctive and instantaneous without the need to apply step by step. You can just enjoy consistently and effortlessly making authentic choices.

WHAT IF I'M AFRAID?

When a decision is the right one, it doesn't necessarily mean it won't scare you a little witless. That's OK. Feeling a little afraid doesn't mean the decision is wrong. It just means the stakes are high and you have a little skin in the game. Good fear feels very close to excitement in the body, it has movement and energy. It is very different from the weight and constriction of an unhelpful decision or the paralysis of panic. You just need to get good at reading the unique distinctions in your own body. I think it was the fabulous Dame Judy Dench that said "it's not about getting rid of the butterflies, it's about getting them to fly in formation." You may never feel the total absence of fear, but if it's the right choice for you, your body knows you have what it takes to make it work. Trust yourself. You can do this.

FEAR OF MISSING OUT

Fear of missing out is an epic problem, particularly in the entrepreneurial community. The next band wagon comes along and everybody hops on board.

I get it, it's easily done. The latest trend, event, craze is alluring, the promises are beautifully packaged and you don't want to be left behind while everyone else is enjoying their place in the sun. This widget, whatever it might be, could be exactly what you need right now. But it's probably not. And here's how I know. If fear of missing out is what's driving you to do something then it's not the right thing, because in an inspired and empowered business, fear does not get to drive!

So when the next opportunity comes along, don't just jump unthinkingly on the band wagon. Remember, you are a free thinker, going your own way. Check it for sense, commercially and emotionally. Do you have time and space for it? Will it feed your vitality? Does it align with your values, does it inspire you, motivate you and support your unique mission?

Avoiding being pulled off track by fear of missing out can be pretty much guaranteed by absorbing yourself in doing what you love. If you're passionate, fulfilled and happy doing what you're doing, there's nothing you're going to miss.

COMPARISON IS THE THIEF OF JOY

If there's one thing that gets in the way of our ability to stay true to our own wisdom and unique path it's comparison. It has the power to drag you down like almost nothing else. The comparing mind is not an empowered one.

Where does comparison take place? Well, social media has to be right up there, doesn't it? It's a breeding ground for comparative insecurities so let's start there. What happens that allows the act of comparison on social media to steal your joy? Sometimes it's so sneaky you might not even be aware of it until hours or even days later, when it's sapped your creative energy and your mojo has got up and gone.

If we pause for a moment to look at the mechanics of what's happening when you are engaged in an unconscious scroll through your Twitter or Instagram feed, it's often a push-me pull-you between taking information in on screen and an internal monologue of negative self talk... you know what I'm talking about, when you see a stunning post and beat yourself up for the poor quality of your own photography, the fact that your flat lays are well...flat. That it should have been you that posted that little snippet of inspiration, gone on that amazing trip or launched that new product. Heck, I've been there, got the t-shirt, am writing the book about it. The point is you probably aren't aware of that comparing voice, just the growing sense of inadequacy. Left unchecked it grows into a demon hell-bent on destroying your motivation and self esteem.

To prevent this pattern of the comparing mind having such a negative and draining effect, you simply need to become more mindful. More aware of your present thoughts and feelings. Noticing when those sneaky thoughts of self-doubt, self-flagellation and negative comparison arise is half the battle.

Start to pay more attention to what you are telling yourself when you see something that might spark comparison. A key flag for whether you're in the comparison mindset, particularly where social media is concerned, is when you start to check

numbers of followers, your own or others. Or when you stop really reading the posts and get lost in thought and lose energy. These are your signals to put the phone down and step away; down that road lies madness, and comfort eating.

Instead, focus your energies on your unique talents, on bringing your individual perspective to the world, on making your own art and being joyful in it. Remind yourself that you are good enough, creative enough, more than enough.

FAILURE

what to do when things get tough

'a tree doesn't grow strong
without the wind'

ELIZABETH CAIRNS

FAILURE

what to do when things get tough

There is no failure. Only opportunities.

There's an expression in the coaching community, "there is no failure, only feedback," and it's been hugely helpful to me over the years. It implies that everything is a process, one of discovery, of incremental improvement. This doesn't mean you're going to get everything right of course. You're inevitably going to make mistakes. You might upset clients, make a poor judgement call or wish you hadn't gone down a particular road. We all get it wrong sometimes. There's a difference between making mistakes and feeling like a failure. How you deal with those blips and your mind-set as you do, is what separates the regular business owner from the Empowered Entrepreneur.

Every failure is an opportunity to learn something.

Every mistake, if dealt with quickly and proactively, doesn't have to compromise on your vitality or be detrimental to your business. Adopting this 'no failure only feedback' mindset can help you reframe problems into opportunities, to efficiently take the learning and move on.

WHEN THINGS GET TOUGH

There will likely come a time in your work when the going gets tough. When it feels like it's not working, maybe to the point where you've had enough. It may be that you've been slogging it out for a fair few years and things just feel staid.

What do you do when things get tough?

There can be a temptation to stay on the treadmill, to keep pushing on through. This is when your inspired work can begin to feel like a job, when what once gave you joy now feels like a burden and something that just has to be done. You start to lose your spontaneity. Maybe the work flow starts to dry up a little. Generally there is a malaise and, if you don't tackle it, it begins to spread beyond the boundaries of your business and affect your wellbeing.

This is a perfect entrepreneurial opportunity. When you are closely connected to your business it is absolutely natural that the shape of that business will shift and even the nature of the work will change entirely. One of the huge benefits of working for yourself and not having all the infrastructure of a large corporation is that you can be nimble, you can flex and adjust to the changing winds and set a new course when you have to.

Sometimes it's just a blip and you need to keep going. What's needed might be a top up of the inspiration banks, some space to work on your business and remind yourself what you love about it, where your strengths lie. Maybe a brand refresh and a few tweaks to your proposition are enough. Remember the power of taking a few days space, away from your usual environment to focus on your business and look at things with fresh eyes. Get the input of industry experts, connect to like minds. Fall in love with your work all over again.

Often when this feeling of malaise has become chronic, the blip is more deep seated. It's a signal for a deeper shift.

This is when you can take time out and away. It doesn't have to be long, for many people, life can't simply stop and you have responsibilities that go beyond those of your clients. The quality of the time is more important than the amount of it. Create space, to discern the new direction and start asking questions. Reconnect with what's important to you, not just your business. Consider using a coach or a third party that can help you explore your inner landscape and reflect back to you some of your thinking. Begin to open yourself up to what's next.

Ask yourself. If you could wave a magic wand and have anything happen in your life and your business right now, what would it be? This gives you insight into your deepest desire.

What is most important to you in your life right now?

This tells you the core values at play, allow these to guide you. Decisions made in support of your values will usually find a way of working out.

What are your deepest gifts and how could you bring them more fully to the world? What brings you joy? What do you stand for? What legacy do you want to leave?

These questions are disruptive, in a good way. They have power. They are opening, seeking, profound. By asking them, you honour yourself and your purpose.

Now you won't necessarily be able to discover the shape of a new business venture from these questions or plan exactly how to make the shift immediately to an alternative lifestyle. But they give you insight, they start to acknowledge the call that you've not been paying attention to. It opens you up to possibilities and lays the foundation for change. It is the habit of the Empowered Entrepreneur to seek to fulfil your deepest callings and desire, to elevate your work to new levels to grow into what's truly possible for you and your business.

If you find yourself at this crossroads, ask yourself...do I just need to revitalise my existing business, or is there something else that is calling me?

FLOW

the path of least resistance

flow

FLOW

the path of least resistance

Flow is both a concept and a state of being that is intimately understood by the Empowered Entrepreneur.

Flow is what occurs when you become absorbed in your creative process, when time is irrelevant and you are seamless with your process, at one with the creating.

Flow is also a way to describe the movement of things at ease and in harmony with the natural order.

You need both flow in the moment when you are absorbed in your work and flow in your life as a whole for you to thrive and achieve potential.

This isn't about kicking back and floating down stream, however. Going with the flow isn't a euphemism for coasting and failing. It's not a passive process. It's an active choice to be in harmony, to find a way of ease that is supported by more than you can always see or put your finger on. Going with the flow means you proactively deal with those things that hold you back and instinctively know which flows, like vitality and inspiration, are most important.

GO WITH THE FLOW

trusting the greater process

Going with the flow might not necessarily be something that feels instinctive to you. Our work culture is geared up to encourage us to push on through, to make things happen, to drive forwards. There is a time for that healthy work ethic, when we need to stay focused, to put in the graft and remain on task until it's done. As an entrepreneur it's likely you have an abundance of that energy which is a great thing, as long as it's not the dominant force all of the time.

If pushing on through is your only mode of operating it comes with risk; loss of perspective, stifling of inspiration, even burnout. As a general guiding principle, the application of continual force in business is an unnecessary waste of energy that can be much better used elsewhere.

To go with the flow is to know that there is a deeper process at work which we might not always be able to control. It's to recognise that there is a natural order to things that facilitates the achievement of your greatest potential. It is a state of being that requires little energy, just an ability to tune in to how things are working and a willingness to go with it.

When you do that, you are working with inspiration and not against it, you are working in harmony and encountering much less resistance. In short, it takes a whole lot less energy, makes things easier and frees you up to enjoy being absorbed in what really matters.

The key thing to bear in mind when going with the flow is that there is a perfect time for everything and, whilst you can influence it, you cannot control it. This is something that happens beyond you as an individual, but that you can fall into rhythm with and benefit from.

Going with the flow is a skill you can master. It requires a sensitivity to your unique creative process, your inner emotional landscape and the external forces that influence. There's an element of trust that comes with going with the flow. Trust that you might not always know exactly what the future holds, trust that if you do the work of staying inspired then the steps will reveal themselves at the right time.

ALIGNING YOUR BUSINESS WITH FLOW
knowing when to wait

The benefits of a go-with-the-flow approach to your work, are abundant. It takes far less energy to relax into a process than anxiously seek to control outcomes all the time. It's easier on your nervous system which ultimately impacts on your overall sense of wellbeing and it actually enables you to get an awful lot more done.

With a driving, forceful approach, your work can become very linear. One thing follows the next and there's little breathing room for processing and assimilation of learning or gestation of new inspired projects. It can also start to fall apart and become very stressful when anyone else is involved in the process. Going with the flow is about recognising that not everything will always work to your own predetermined time-scales. So when a client isn't ready to begin work, a project stalls or you're not getting the responses you need, pause. Forcing those things and desperately trying to nail everything down just expends energy, drains vitality and gets you no where fast. There might be other pieces of the puzzle needed before things can move on. You may just not be able to see them yet. You need to be able to adapt, stay fluid, ride the next wave of inspiration.

Going with the flow in action is relatively straight forward once you get a feel for it. Predominantly it's about knowing when to wait. About intuiting whether something isn't working because it's the wrong direction or simply a matter of wrong timing. When you hit a wall and can't move something forward, ask yourself if it's the right time for this to happen? You may well discover it's not.

Sometimes the wait will be a short one and things will align quicker than you might think. Sometimes things are in suspended animation for what may seem like an uncomfortably long time.

This is when you can follow the threads of your inspiration to what naturally needs to happen next. You also need to manage your emotional responses to the situation so they don't get in the way. Being gentle with yourself is key. Watch out for when irritation or frustration show up and know that feeding those beasts just takes energy away from where you want to go. Trust. Ultimately if something doesn't work out, it's probably not right, and that's ok. Provided you stay deeply rooted in your authentic work, things are exactly as they should be.

So when it feels like external forces are resisting you, it's a signal to pause, become conscious of your approach, tune in to your inner wisdom, follow your inspiration and realign with the greater flow.

The ability to do this seamlessly, without wasting too much energy just comes with practice. It takes a willingness to suspend your usual patterns of forcing things through to completion and of course that all important trust, in yourself, the value of your work and the greater process.

FLOW IN YOUR CREATIVE PROCESS
the gateway to your best work

The creative process is enhanced by being in flow and a precursor to doing your best work. The flow I'm referring to here is an altered state of consciousness, where you feel at your best and your performance is greatly enhanced.

When in flow your brain is flooded with neuro-transmitters like dopamine, serotonin and endorphins, hence the enhanced mood. Your sense of time is altered and you have amplified cognitive performance, in simple terms you become smarter.

Flow can be experienced in anything you are doing. You may recognise it when you are giving a presentation and you know you're on fire, when you're absorbed with your children, playing music, sports, martial arts, yoga, watching nature, dancing, painting...

When I experience flow, particularly when writing it's as if I have access to a whole stream of information that wasn't there before. My hand moves the pen faster than I can write and I'm not really aware of the thoughts as they flow through me. I simply need to keep up with the writing or typing. It feels good. It's energising yet relaxing in my body, there's no tension.

Flow is something you can train. You just need to create the conditions for it.

In my experience, maintaining high vitality enhances flow. Both the likelihood of accessing it in the first place and how long I can sustain it. I suspect it has something to do with how taxing flow is on the reserves of our body. It uses up vast amounts of enzymes to produce the neurotransmitters which drains our protein and mineral stores.

Space is a pre-requisite to flow. As I've said in *Space*, you need to give yourself the time in your creative work to step away from a project. To allow your brain to switch off from conscious processing and synergise information. You also need to create space at the end of a period of flow to adequately recover for the next stint. To restore the body's reserves and prepare yourself for the more challenging effort of priming your brain for more input.

Impatiens: Bringing rest and easing
tension when you find it hard to
wait, or are quick to temper.

PRIMING YOUR BRAIN FOR FLOW

To prime for flow you need to lay the groundwork. You need to give your brain the information it needs to produce the work you desire. This is probably the hardest part of the process and can take the most time.

It's also personally where I encounter the most resistance.

The priming for flow for this book took years. I spent time learning my craft, experimenting, coaching, listening, working with entrepreneurs from all over the world. I spent time journalling, exploring my inner landscape. I followed my passions: read books, attended seminars, watched ted talks, attended courses and watched videos. I didn't know at the time I was priming for flow but that's exactly what it was.

Towards the end of this project, in the last 18 months I was priming more deliberately. Loading my brain with the specific information I wanted at my fingertips when it came time to write. Brainstorming, planning, drafting, noting, listening, learning, observing, reviewing. I expected resistance and was ready for it. Using the tools I have learnt to trust the process and keep showing up to achieve the goal.

When the final writing phase came I could enjoy the rewards of experiencing flow more often. The joy that comes with ease of writing and the culmination of a decade of work. Intimate with my own creative process, I could enjoy cycling through those necessary phases to get the job done: Priming, space, flow, rest. Priming, space, flow, rest.

Getting into a flow state at will doesn't take years of practice, just a conscious decision to create the conditions.

SIMPLE STEPS TO FINDING FLOW

Set your goal Decide on your project or piece of work.

Raise your vitality Nurture your body with good food and hydration, avoiding alcohol and stimulants. Reduce your stress and get the sleep you need.

Practice the discrete skills and rudiments of your craft until you can do them without thinking.

Follow your passion and your inspiration. Load your brain with what it needs.

Create the space to do your best work.

Enjoy flow.

WHAT TO DO WHEN FLOW ELUDES YOU

Does it feel like flow is eluding you? Does it seem that you neither have that time stopping, utterly absorbing, awe inspiring experience of in-the-moment-flow, nor that greater sense that things are going smoothly and serendipity is on your side? If this is your experience it may be a call to even deeper levels of authenticity in your work, to take time to be still and to listen to the quiet murmurs of your soul, whatever form that takes.

Enabling flow in your creative process is helped hugely by an irreverent attitude. One that enjoys the unfolding, the not knowing, one that seeks ways to bring lightness and humour and ease to events. In other words, don't take it all too seriously. After all, the opposite of play is not work, the opposite of play is depression. Allow yourself the space and time to be playful, trusting that it's all part of the process.

flow

FLOW-DRIVEN MARKETING
a pull not push process

So you've written a great book, created an awesome product, designed an e-course, workshop...any new offering that will really serve your clients. What do you do next? The tendency is to be pulled into thinking that the obvious next step is to start selling whatever it is you've created. It's not.

Hear me out. I'm not suggesting you bury your manuscript under a pile of papers on your desk never to see the light of day, but the sales strategies of old where you have to flog, flog, flog the living daylights out of it have given way to an altogether more enjoyable and elegant way of aligning people with your product.

Yes you need to get it out there. Put it in a place where people can find it. Let people know it's there. Talk with passion on your chosen platform about the value this new widget creates and what a great /challenging / inspiring ...fill in the blank time you had putting it all together, but don't be lulled into thinking that this should be the sole focus of your work now. When you are running an inspired business, marketing is built into the process and happens naturally each time you are inspired and create new work. Your work is to create new work and in the creation of that, your previous endeavours get fed by that energy and continue to grow.

There is a point at which the energy naturally created by the bringing to life of something wonderful shifts and then it takes on a life of its own. There's a point at which you need to let go a little, or a lot. It's almost like motherhood. You birth this wonderful baby, it's out in the world and needs care and attention, a little guidance. Then it begins to find its own feet and, with the occasional steer and support, it goes out into the world and makes a life for itself, often one you could never had envisaged in the time before it was born. If you can let it go, it can travel the world, doing great things. But only if you take the next step and keep creating.

What often happens, particularly with things we have created, is we get lulled into thinking that our creative work is done and we can rest on our laurels. We stop innovating, stop growing and place all our energy and attention on that one piece of work. We're still selling the hell out of what we've made so it feels like we are still working, but in reality we're not because our real work lies in using our creative gifts and talents to bring more into the world. As a creative entrepreneur, if you stop creating you shut off one of the most valuable marketing processes for your business, the energy of new work.

Creating new work: an inspired marketing strategy

Let's take writing a book as an example. You write the book, people like it, in fact they love it. There's a buzz about it on social media, sales do really well initially and it might even be a best seller. You're thrilled, naturally, it's a wonderful thing. You are inspired and begin your next project. But soon book sales begin to die down a little as they naturally do when something is no longer on everyones' lips and something else has caught the attention of your audience. This can create a tinge of anxiety, mild panic even. You get pulled away from the new project and start to worry about sales and how to make more of them.

You panic post or panic blog in the hope of generating that buzz again and it may work a little but it still feels a little desperate. You begin to notice all the comments from those people who aren't buying the book, their excuses, their reluctance and it sows a seed of doubt. "Have I done enough, how can I convert these unwilling people? What can I do to change their mindset and get them to buy the book?" This is a totally natural progression of thought but it takes energy, quite a lot of energy, and it's problem focused. Each time you get your monthly statement of book sales you are a little anxious. The number of sales has unwittingly become the only measure of success that counts. You no longer notice the other markers for success. The difference our book is making to our readership, for example. It feels a little draining. That glow and positive energy you created in writing and launching has been dulled and it's hard to find the momentum to pick up something new.

This is only natural. It's easy to get caught up in the pushing and promotion and selling of your work and to get disheartened if you don't get the results you were expecting. There's a way of marketing and approaching the process that is more energy efficient. One that harnesses this energy of inspired vitality and isn't as clunky as the make product, sell product model of operating. It's more elegant, there's a slight shift of focus and it feels more enlivening.

The scenario of the empowered entrepreneur who has created her book, course, product...fill in the blank, plays out something like this:

An empowered way to market your business

Your book is out there and is well received. You do your initial flurry of marketing and all is well, initial sales figures are pretty good. You've moved on to another project. Then book sales take a dip. You realise this is natural, after all you've been focused on other projects, projects that have also been well received by your audience. Instead of panicking, you remember that a book is a long term project, sales will grow over time. You relax and remind yourself that it would be helpful to do some marketing for it when you feel inspired to. You also give some focused attention to the types of things that might be useful to add value to your audience in relation to the book. What would it help them to understand? How does it add value? And you open up the possibility of opportunities to present themselves. Then you get back to work.

You focus your energies on your creative work, your next project, serving your clients well. Momentum builds, you attract a wider audience to your work, they notice your book, sales grow organically. Your creative work has really fuelled your entrepreneurial fire and that buzz is created again. An opportunity presents itself for you to be interviewed for a podcast to talk about the impact of your work and it's the perfect audience to talk about your book. Sales peak again. The whole process is organic, flowing, enjoyable and positive.

Where you place your attention and the nature of that attention has made all the difference to the outcome. You've avoided a whole lot of stress that easily spirals downwards, killing the naturally productive and attractive energy and instead continued to create and feed the energy of a brand that has momentum, is meaningful and is truly serving your audience and yourself.

When you are in the flow of doing your best creative work, you become very attractive. If your marketing efforts are a natural extension of that inspiration and enthusiasm they have so much more power.

flow

THE ESSENCE OF
FLOW DRIVEN MARKETING

Making a real difference to just one individual can have a huge impact on the shape of your business. One person who has received genuine benefit will fly your flag more congruently, passionately and influentially, than a bucket load of scattergun social media posts. Flow driven marketing isn't calculated, it's inspired. It happens as a genuine extension of the energy and excitement you create in the making or delivery of your product or service.

Doing your best work, focusing on the value to your audience of what you do and being genuine and timely in your enthusiasm lies at the heart of flow driven marketing.

SEASONAL FLOW

harnessing the cycles of nature in your work

There is a season for everything, a rhythm that we can work with, or against. Each season has an energy that, once you recognise and understand it, you can utilise to grow your business and further your creative development.

I look at seasonal flow a little like nested Russian dolls. There are seasons within seasons within seasons, all fitting harmoniously together to create a whole and yet each complete within itself. The first seasons we look to of course are those played out in nature. Four distinct phases that cycle round and round, reliably, effortlessly and according to their own rhythm.

Winter, the cold, dark, retreating, processing, restorative energy where the earth recycles the dead matter, draws back into the shadows and things are laid bare.

Spring, that rising, quick, light and motivating energy of awakening to possibilities of new life and beginnings.

Summer, that warming, abundant easy energy where nature blooms and comes into its own seemingly without effort and we enjoy the literal fruits of our labours from early spring.

Early Autumn when the abundance of the late harvest is ripe for the picking. The animals are productively preparing for the winter months to come, seeds are created in preparation for the following spring and nature is beginning to shed what is no longer necessary.

I see these seasons reflected in business in a number of ways.

Start ups with the energy of Spring make a lot happen in a short time to get things off the ground. More established companies that have laid the groundwork may take things at a slower pace, more reflective of summer or late autumn. They enjoy seeing the culmination of their efforts in a sustainable and profitable business and there is a little more time to kick back and relax. Businesses that have had their time, are drawing to a close, making way for new endeavours fall into winter and so the cycle continues.

The seasons can also be reflected in your creative projects and business offerings. If you have multiple facets to your business or a lot of projects on the go you are likely to be in different seasons for each one. At the completion of a project, like launching a new product line, completing a commission or finalising a piece of client work there would naturally be a winter-like phase of review and reflection where the seeds of new ideas can start to make themselves known. Spring time fits new endeavours or projects in full swing might require a great deal of sustained energy and attention. Summer and early autumn contains those established offerings that are, relatively, effortless to maintain and likely form the bedrock of your business.

The Brand Stylist, a business founded by creative entrepreneur Fiona Humberstone, is one that helps us see this concept of nested seasons in action. At any given time Fiona will have a number of projects and offerings that form her work as a whole. One in Spring, at the forefront of her creative edge, where she is gaining new insights, applying lots of focussed energy, constantly seeking inspiration and producing a phenomenal amount of work towards her end goal. This might be creative direction for a new client, a new online course or perhaps writing a new book. Then there will be others that she has brought to completion and delivered. These take the more gentle energy of summer to maintain and include past books, ongoing online courses, workshops and the like. These may require a quick dip into winter to review and revise and a very short flurry of productive early autumn energy at the time they are delivered again. There will also be one or two offerings each year that she has outgrown, creatively or professionally, and these fit into winter. These she releases to make space for the germination of new inspired ideas that will elevate her offering and keep pushing her creative edge.

At any given time it's easy to see which projects are in which season and how they all sing along together to create a broad and bountiful offering. One that fulfils both Fiona's creative potential and her desire to run a profitable, sustainable enterprise.

Notice where your business sits and which of your offerings are in which kind of energy at the moment. If everything is in spring all at the same time it might be a high energy, incredibly intense and productive time but recognise that this level of activity isn't one that you can or should maintain for extended periods. It's simply not sustainable and is a fast road to burnout if you try. The seasons cycle and so can you.

DANDELION

'a humble reminder of change
as a constant and how bud,
bloom and seed can coexist'

ELIZABETH CAIRNS

Lean into the unfolding, trust the process and each step will reveal itself at the right time.

THE EVOLVING NATURE OF INSPIRED WORK

Your business evolves with your creative edge. What you are inspired to create and bring into the world is what leads the direction of your work. There is a flow to the creative process and an energy that you can harness to drive and shape your business. Think of it like a beautiful fern unfolding, revealing each frond as it goes.

As an Empowered Entrepreneur, you are not bound by convention, other than those you choose to create, and you have the freedom to shape your business or businesses around those things that light you up and you feel compelled to do. I don't know about you, but I think that's pretty exciting.

It is important to realise that your authentic work, as a natural extension of your unique skills and talents, will shift and grow as you do. You need to create space to allow that to happen and be open to the signs when it's time for change.

The expectation that you may be employed in the same work, or even the same type of work for life as an entrepreneur is perhaps misguided. That's not to say you can't have one true calling and follow it through, and that of course may last a lifetime, but the expression of it will naturally evolve. Change is inevitable. It's one of the fundamental rules of nature and we must learn how to dance with it if we are to fulfil our potential and enjoy the process.

Getting stuck in a rut or taking the predictable slow and steady path isn't the destiny of an empowered and inspired entrepreneur. That might seem a little scary or very exciting but, in my experience, it's the truth of it. Living an empowered and inspired life is much much more dynamic and evolutionary than that. There is a lot more happening than we can safely and predictably control. The skills we need master in this arena aren't everyones' cup of tea but they make for a deeper, richer experience of ourselves and our work.

There is a different quality to work that is authentically evolving with us, versus that which is simply in the box of a job for life. There is creativity, dynamism, flow, serendipity if you will. It's where the magic happens.

GETTING
IT DONE

the work ethic of an empowered entrepreneur

GETTING IT DONE

the work ethic of an empowered entrepreneur

You understand the need for space in your inspired business and how prioritising vitality provides fuel for your work. With all this talk of space and wellbeing, you might be fooled into thinking there's no real work involved at all, that nothing ever really gets done.

Far from it. There is no shortage of action in an inspired business with an Empowered Entrepreneur at the helm. The point of all that foundation is to ensure that when you take action it's the right thing, at the right time, in the right direction. When it comes to it, the Empowered Entrepreneur knows exactly what it takes to get the job done. So in this part of the book we are going to address your work ethic and kicking into touch the things that get in the way of productive, effective work.

TIME

you have more power over it than you think

Time is important. You know that. It's your one finite, irreplaceable resource. Once you've spent it, it's gone. There's no banking it for later.

Time is often experienced as something you feel you have, or not. What if you could see it differently? Once you recognise that you have a partnership with time and that you have power in that relationship, it makes all the difference.

First you must get really intimate with this partner and see its true value. Part of knowing the true value of time, is to let your mortality really sink in.

Accepting the frailty of the human condition isn't always a yellow brick road of a journey, but it is necessary. It doesn't have to involve a painful wake up call or be a gloomy slide towards your demise. Simply a recognition. Allow it to penetrate and work its motivating magic.

Once you have that respect for time in your bones, you can work on honing the skills that need mastering to get the most from your relationship.

Time travel with intention is a skill you can use to shape your work.

Visioning for the future, reflecting and learning from the past, being powerfully present, are all things the Empowered Entrepreneur does as a matter of course.

VISIONING
a practical way to shape your future

You business needs vision to grow. It needs a sense of future, of possibility, a shape and a direction. Crafting a vision is something a lot of people seem to struggle with, but vision isn't something you either have or you don't. Visioning is a skill you can hone. If you can create a picture in your mind then you can create a vision, and in 20 years of doing this work I haven't yet met someone who can't.

It's often been said that if you can see it, you can achieve it and I truly believe this. Your ideas for your business, your plans for the future, aren't just teasing, mocking, false promises that aren't within your reach. If you have conceived of it, then it is totally possible for you. In fact I can pretty much guarantee that even if you think your vision is huge and big and scary, it's only a fraction of what you are actually capable of.

It doesn't really matter what your vision is, as long as it's authentic to you. It's how you use it that makes the difference between whether it becomes a reality or not.

What future do you want to create?
If you could paint a bright and beautiful future for your business, what would it look like? What is the vision you want to create?

If you really want a vision to work for you, you have to make it tangible and internalise it so that it motivates you to action. Take some time to capture that in what ever format works for you. Vision boards are great for this and, of course, written goals work too.

Bringing your vision to life
What often gets missed when crafting a vision is live visioning. Live visioning is the ability to play a movie or see the image of your vision in your mind's eye and create a whole body response to it. It is your visceral response to what you see in your imagination that provides the motivation for the goal and sows the seeds of magic.

For a vision to work best, you have to be able to call it up at will and make it tangible. This is what makes it motivating and bridges the gap between thought and action. The desire to achieve it needs to felt in your bones.

To many entrepreneurs, those who are really good at seeing their visions through to completion, this is an unconscious process that happens naturally. For some it takes a little more conscious effort until it become a habit.

The practice of live visioning

Imagine the vision of your future as if it's a movie or an image playing out in front of you. If you are in the movie or picture make sure you are dissociated in the image. Meaning you can either see your face or the back/side of your head, rather than seeing everything through your own eyes. Dissociated visions are more compelling because you want to move towards them. If you are already in it, it's as if it's already happening and it won't have so much power.

Whilst looking at the image through your mind's eye, notice how your body feels. You are aiming for something that makes you feel amazing, perhaps excited, perhaps inspired but definitely motivated. When you look at your future you want it to feel good.

Now play around with the qualities of that movie or image as if you are an editor. You are aiming to tweak your movie until the feelings of desire, clarity and confidence associated with it are enhanced.

You might add more light, make the image moving or still, add a soundtrack, play around with perspective or positioning in the frame. You might enhance the colour, focus or depth of field.

Experiment with the distance the image is from you in the present moment. Push it way away into the future and notice how your feelings change. Bring it right up close to you and see what shifts. There will be a sweet spot that feels close enough to be certain that it's going to happen but far enough away that it's motivating. Play around until you find just the right edit and place in time for your vision to sit.

It is worth taking the time to craft a vision that lifts you, inspires you and helps to shape the course of your life and your work in meaningful ways. It can really help to include a wider perspective, too. Seeing how your goals for your business fit seamlessly with the other important aspects of your life help make the vision more ecologically sound for you. This makes it much more likely to happen.

Giving your vision the right time-frame

The time frame for your vision will make a difference. Long term goals and hugely aspirational visions that are set waaaay off in the future may work for some, but often they're just not close enough to focus on. They can result in feelings of overwhelm and paralysis.

Give yourself permission to set your own timeframe for your vision. If you can only see six months or even three ahead that's absolutely fine.

It just needs to be far enough in the future to pull you towards it and close enough to feel almost within reach. There's a sweet spot for motivation that's worth playing around with until you get it right.

If you know you struggle staying true to your vision or motivation wanes, you can deliberately make live visioning part of your daily routine. If you do a visioning exercise once a year and then step away from it thinking it's done, you're missing out on so much of the power of it.

Create an all-singing all-dancing, bright, colourful, beautiful internal movie of your desires for your business. Build in the habit of visiting it every day. See if that doesn't kick some of the procrastination or lack of motivation into touch.

Live Visioning doesn't need to be reserved for the big goals and annual business planning. It's something you can use daily to enhance your sense of control and capability over upcoming events. Envisioning that meeting going well, seeing yourself nailing that talk or presentation, watching your perfect response to that tricky client, needy friend, challenging family member, any situation can benefit.

Live visioning is rehearsal for life that really makes a difference. High performing athletes use it, world class performers use it, expectant mothers preparing for birth use it, and Empowered Entrepreneurs are masters at it.

'With vision you get to define the shape of
your work and the course of your life.'

ELIZABETH CAIRNS

'Simplicity is the ultimate form of
sophistication'

LEONARDO DE VINCI

CREATIVE CURSES

the antithesis to productivity

Over the years of working with creative entrepreneurs around the world I have noticed similar traits that often get in the way of effective and brilliant work. I've come to fondly call them the creative curses. It's useful to address them if you are to be as productive and efficient in your business as possible.

Headless chicken syndrome Running around being busy, with very little focus or actual productive work. When you get so little reward for all that energy you are spending.

Overwhelm Paralysing, energy draining, mind boggling, head fogging exhausting overwhelm. When there's just too much of everything.

Overwork Not knowing when or how to stop. The working day goes on and on. There's no time or space and there seems to be no way out of the trap.

Action paralysis When you just can't get going, your plans never seem to get started or followed through to completion. This often comes with an ideas glut, where there are plenty of thoughts but either no energy. no time or no confidence to put them in to action.

Finally, dear old *Ostrich*, which involves a whole load of avoidance and procrastination. You know things aren't quite right but you just stick your head in the sand and hope everything will go away.

You'll be thrilled to know you can experience them all (aren't you the lucky one), or have a particular predisposition to one or another as part of your creative process. I wonder which is your favourite?

Falling foul to these pests seems to be par for the course for many entrepreneurs. Rather than beat yourself up for it, let's explore some practical strategies for taming the little beasts.

BUSY VS PRODUCTIVE
the curse of the headless chicken

The curse of the headless chicken is to be busy but rarely productive. I'm sure you've had those odd days when it all seems crazy busy but you don't get much done. Too many of them and you can start to feel out of control, like you're not making headway and instead just end up falling foul of those other pests, overwork and overwhelm.

Feeling busy, but not necessarily productive, can often be the result of letting others dictate your priorities, not knowing when to say no, or being driven by fear of missing out rather than your own authentic goals.

Headless chicken can also be the result of not enough planning and forethought and unrealistic expectations of what you can manage with the time that you have.

The feeling of 'busy' is markedly different from the feeling of 'productivity'. Busy often comes with a kind of frantic, almost hysterical edge. A lot of excess movement and dissipated energy that leaves you a bit spent and empty at the end of the day.

Productivity, on the other hand, is focused; it still creates energy but it's much more contained. It has perspective and purpose and the feeling at the end of a productive phase is one of achievement and satisfaction.

MAKING THE SWITCH FROM BUSY TO PRODUCTIVE

Keep your eye on the bigger picture What is it you want to achieve overall? What are the smaller steps that will bring you closer to it?

Streamline and simplify What is clogging up your day unnecessarily? What can you say no to? What can you delegate? What really doesn't need to be done? You will have started to explore this earlier on in *Doing Vital Work*.

Keep your perfectionist in check What is taking you longer than it needs to? If you have perfectionist tendencies you can easily make a job that could take an hour, last a whole morning.

Don't over commit This question is worth asking more than once...What are you doing because you think you should? If you're just keeping up appearances, drop it. You are enough just as you are.

Decide what's most important You simply cannot do it all. Take the time to be clear about what is most important to you and why. Prioritise that over everything else.

OVERWHELM
taking back the reins

Headless chicken syndrome can easily lead to overwhelm and it can be crippling for any business owner. It is something that needs tackling in the moment when it strikes and at the root to prevent it overtaking you in the future. The antithesis to overwhelm is space and hopefully by now you're fully on board with the benefits of making space.

DEALING WITH OVERWHELM IN THE MOMENT

In the moments when overwhelm hits you it can feel well, totally overwhelming. It can have a debilitating effect on your progress. Having a strategy to quickly and easily move yourself into a different state so you can begin to address the root cause will help.

1. Look up Raise your eyes above the horizon and allow them to fall into soft focus. Peripheral vision helps calm the central nervous system and immediately gives you an expanded sense of space.

2. Step out Get yourself outside in the fresh air and get your body moving. The energy of overwhelm is heavy and gets stuck in the body. Moving, particularly brisk walking, can start to shift your thinking out of that stuck state and into a more proactive, problem solving mode.

3. Look out Find somewhere with an expansive view of the surrounding landscape. A wide open view signals to your mind that you have more room to think. Your eye is drawn to the horizon again which is instantly relaxing, whilst wide open spaces allow more light in which boosts your mood and helps bring clarity.

4. Step up Remind yourself that you're in control then take action. Overwhelm will usually stop you in your tracks and you don't want that inertia to settle in. Do something, however small, to move forwards and take some control back. Free writing in your journal can be a great first step, or writing a list or action plan. Keep things moving.

Addressing the root of overwhelm

Once you're out of the full state of overwhelm you can then start to address the root. It's likely a cycle that repeats for you so the process is simple, look back, look forwards, step up.

Look back over recent events to notice when the overwhelm started to take hold and what led up to it, it's likely a repeating pattern. Notice at what point you knew it was time to be overwhelmed. Then look further back. There will have been a point at which it could have been avoided, pay attention to that.

Look forward Take a look at your diary over the coming days weeks and months. Is there enough space built in to prevent it happening again? What do you need to put in place to reduce the likelihood of overwhelm and help you feel back in control? If there's just too much going on, your priority becomes discerning what takes priority. Focussing your energy on finding out what's most important rather than fire fighting will help tame the beast.

Forward planning really helps kick overwhelm into touch, so build in regular space to raise your head above the busyness of the everyday and look to the future.

Step up Now you have more awareness about your unique causes of overwhelm don't go all ostrich. Take the action you need to protect yourself from it in the future. Remember to be gentle with yourself too. If it's a familiar habit it may take a little while to shift but shift it will and you will feel liberated when it does.

OVERWORK

the road to burnout is paved with good intentions

All work and no play makes jack a dull boy... and the business owner sick. You might not even realise you are overworking. Your state of exhaustion might be so chronic that you've come to treat it as normal. Overworking is so prevalent in our culture that it's come to be expected. Well, not for the Empowered Entrepreneur!

Knowing when to stop is something that might take a little practice, but knowing your limitations and respecting them will make running your business much more sustainable. Working with healthier boundaries around your time will also improve your vitality and overall wellbeing, which you know is better for business. You cannot run your business if you are on your knees.

Tackling overwork by clarifying your niche

Overwork can often be the result of good intentions but if you are trying to be all things to all people in your business and attempting to keep everyone happy, it comes at a cost.

No-one gets the best from you and you are run ragged in the process. If this is happening it suggests that you might not have defined your niche clearly enough. Taking time to craft your unique offering and really get specific about who you are targeting will help.

The person prone to chronic overwork is one who is often very capable and who sees the needs of others and is driven to meet them.

When you are in this chronically overworked state it can be really difficult to see the wood from the trees but be assured, there is another way to grow your business, a better way that sustains you as well as others.

OAK

'There is a more elegant way of doing
business, one that sustains you as well as
those you serve.'

ELIZABETH CAIRNS

Spot the signals and heed the warning

To get out of the bondage of overwork you need to learn to listen to your body,
recognise the signals of when you are taking it too far. Keep front of mind your
mission and your desires, the whole picture of the life you want to create for
yourself. Having a graceful and respectful way to put down a boundary for yourself
and say "no!" will really help and we will tackle that shortly.

ACTION PARALYSIS
when you just can't get going

There can be a pendulum swing from overwork or overwhelm to the place where action eludes you, when you just can't get going. This can be an acute state where you've got a glut of ideas and plenty of thoughts but very little action or a chronic state where you just lack lustre and aren't able to get things off the ground or follow things through.

Getting out of the land of the fairies

Being in this state can feel a bit like your energy and your mind has wandered off to the land of the fairies. Everything is just floating about and has no real substance, nothing is solid, there's no firm direction, just thoughts and ideas swirling around. The fastest antidote is grounding, getting your energy back into your body, so you can start to move it forward with purpose.

Grounding is straightforward. Anything that gets you in touch with your body will ground you. Eating, dancing, walking, sex, singing…try them all. Better still if you can do them barefoot with your feet in the grass.

Once you're back in your body then you can start to make sense of things, you can feel your way forwards. Your powers of discernment are more available to you. Ask yourself what is most important. If it's a glut of ideas you are faced with, write them all out. Look at each one in turn and use the *Art of Discernment*, feel your way through them. Which ones feel lighter, more free, more inspiring? Which one gives you the strongest pull? Once you know your direction, you can plan for action. What's the next small step you need to take to make this happen? And the one after that? One step at a time, the inertia shifts, and you're back in your flow.

Elm: Support for when
work is overwhelming.

TAMING THE OSTRICH
ways to avoid avoidance

Avoiding things never feels great, does it? Like an ostrich with its head in the sand, it leaves you feeling a bit vulnerable, but it can be a common pattern for an entrepreneur.

Whether it shows up as procrastination or denial, those with ostrich tendencies can find it very difficult to face up to things or get the important things done.

If this feels familiar, take heart. Even the most stubborn procrastination can be put to bed and with a shift of mindset and some simple strategies up your sleeve, you can get those tasks nailed.

Addressing your deepest fear
"Our deepest fear is not that we are inadequate, our deepest fear is that we are powerful beyond measure. It is our light, not our darkness, that most frightens us and playing small does not serve the world." I love this quote by Marianne Williamson, it really shows an understanding of the human psyche.

There are so many reasons we procrastinate. It can be paralysing, frustrating and irritating. As Marianne suggests, part of procrastination is about being fearful to step into your power and really own what you are capable of. If this is the case, you may find you are procrastinating on those things that are really important to you; the book, the new project, starting a business, starting a family. It's easy to procrastinate on those thing that have real meaning for you and enable you to keep playing small.

This type of procrastination, I call resistance.

246

Dealing with resistance

It's as if we are resisting our true purpose and, if this kind of procrastination strikes, it's likely a good signal that you're on the right track. All you need do is recognise that. Start to own it and stop making it so big and so scary. One of the ways to do that is to make the whole thing feel smaller in your mind. Downplay the significance. Break it down into more manageable pieces. You can trick your unconscious mind. If your mind is thinking "this thing is so big, so important, it's my life's work, it could change everything, it's so hard" of course you're not going to do it, you're probably going to be scared witless. But if you tell yourself "oh, it's just this little thing that I'm doing, it's fairly straight forward, I've just got to take these little steps and I know what needs to happen next, it's just a bit of writing..." the whole thing instantly feels more manageable. The aim is to reduce its significance to the same level as something you would do as a matter of course.

Emphasise the value to drive motivation

On the flip side, you may be putting things off because you don't realise how important they are in the bigger picture of things.

When that is the case, you need to emphasise the value rather than reduce it.

There might be things that are really essential to your thriving business, like looking at the financials, or doing your tax return, or sorting out your website, that you are resisting and not treating as important. Lots of people do. That's because you're not looking at them in relation to the grand scheme of things. When you examine the value of something to your overall mission and direction for your business, the motivation to do it appears. If you zoom out and look at the wider benefits of having all of that stuff in order, you'll find you have more drive to get them done.

Act

Procrastination doesn't exist when you take action. To beat it, therefore, all you need to do is do something. As soon as you are taking action, in the direction of where you want to go, you are no longer procrastinating. One of the quickest ways to tackle a goal you are putting off is to write down the next thing you could do to make it happen, one small simple thing, then go and do that. Don't waste time worrying if it is exactly the right thing, just do it. Then write down the next thing and do that, and so on. You'll soon pick up momentum and a flow will develop. Your sense of priority will start to emerge and before long, you'll have cracked it. The point is to pick one very small thing and do it, right now.

Eat the frog first

Brian Tracey has a great approach to dealing with that tendency to put things off and he writes about it in his book 'Eat the Frog.'

Eat the Frog is based on the concept that if you were to eat a frog for breakfast, the chances are that not much else is likely to happen in the day that is going to be worse than eating that frog.

Scenario one: Eat the frog first and you've already won the day. Set yourself up for things to get even better.

Scenario two: Leave the frog sat on your plate, watching you all day. Go off and do 20 other things that aren't really that important. Knowing the frog is there, waiting to be eaten, is just going to drain your energy and drive you nuts.

Eat the frog invites you to do the thing that scares you or is most difficult, first. If you find that what you are procrastinating on is lurking at the back of your mind and draining your energy then the 'eat the frog' approach is the one for you.
Bon Apetit!

BREAK IT DOWN UNTIL IT'S EASY

You may procrastinate because you think it's going to be hard or it feels too difficult.

If that's the case, then you need to break it down into manageable steps that you know are achievable for you. My husband is a master at this. Even my drive to get things done pales into insignificance next to the productivity fiend that is my husband. Mike knows a thing or two about getting things done and has his time management absolutely nailed.

To give you a flavour of it, I'll take you back to 2015. That year my crazy husband set himself the goal of writing a million words of original fiction, self publishing 15 books (from scratch) and vlogging about it every day for a year. He managed it. It's fair to say that he knows a thing or two about getting things done.

One of the things I got him to adopt was TATT's; Timed, Achievable, Tickable Tasks. Basically a tick list that you work through with a timer.

TACKLING TASKS WITH TATTS

Take something that feels massive and unwieldy and *break it down into smaller, 20 minute tasks* that you write down in a list. You don't have to know in which order they should be done to begin with, just write them down. When it comes time to work, set your time for 20 minutes. *Pick a task that makes sense and do it.* Without distraction, without hesitation just focus only on that task until the timer goes off. Repeat.

I recommend *no more than three TATT's in a row* before taking a break. Until you get used to it, TATT's work best if each one doesn't just run into the next. Give each task within that first hour, a slightly different focus. *Novelty helps with attention.*

Your brain will work within the timeframe it is given and you may be surprised at just how much you can get done in 20 minutes with acute focus. Dealing with emails can be a TATT, writing the copy for your home page, pulling together a bank of images for social media, a mid morning yoga break, story boarding a presentation, brainstorming a new venture. TATT's can be anything as long as they are achievable within 20 minutes and done to a timer.

Just three hyper focused TATT's an hour, three hours a day gives you *nine useful things achieved and off your to do list.* How does that compare to your average morning?

Any big project like creating and launching a new training programme or publishing 15 books can be tackled like this.

THE EMPOWERED NO

the skill of putting down a healthy boundary.

Your ability to create space, to prevent overwhelm, to avoid overwork and to take empowered ownership of your life requires that you master an essential skill - The Empowered No.

Without it you can easily find yourself overrun by responsibilities, burdens and a to-do list as long as your arm. There is an art to saying no, which, when perfected, radically changes the landscape of both your work and your wider life.

The ability to say no, to put down a boundary and hold it, is something many people struggle with, so don't worry if you find it hard, you're not alone.

As a business owner, there are so many things you need to be able to confidently say no to; opportunities that don't serve your business, meetings that are a waste of time, social media noise, that extra cup of coffee when what your body really needs is rest, the friend who abuses your time and your generosity, the family member unable to stand on their own two feet...Everywhere you turn there are things vying for your attention, your time and your skills and you simply do not have the capacity for it all.

Attempting to achieve everything means you get pulled in too many different directions and that eventually leads to you getting pulled apart. Rather than draining vital energy by trying to please everyone you can channel it more usefully into fulfilling work.

Protect your reputation

The inability to say no can also potentially be the most damaging thing for your personal and professional brand. When you can't say 'no', you say yes to the wrong things, or agree to something and then at the last minute either make excuses and pull out, or end up doing it grudgingly. All this takes far more energy, effort, time and cost than it ever needed to in the first place. To be successful, you need a brand that people can rely on. That reliability hinges on your ability to turn down those things that aren't right for you.

Even if you do manage to fulfil your commitments to others, there is still the risk that you end up burnt out, sick, tired and, in the end, unable to meet even the most fundamental of your commitments. Ultimately that doesn't serve your business, your clients, or those you care about.

It can be more generous to say no

Saying no often feels hard, particularly if you are generous by nature and concerned for the welfare of those around you. This might dupe you into taking on responsibilities that quite simply aren't yours to take on. It can also mean that you fail to see when things that were once perfectly aligned with your purpose and skills are no longer what best serves you or your clients.

You might avoid saying no for so many reasons. It feels uncomfortable, you don't want to offend, you don't want to appear to be hard, uncaring or unkind, you have a genuine desire to serve and make things better. You can do that simple thing that has been asked of you, so, automatically, you assume that you should do it.

What if you believed that, by saying no, you were actually doing the best possible service to those you care about? What if you believed that you could hold a boundary and still be a genuinely lovely person doing their best? What if saying no wasn't perceived as selfish but as one of the most generous things you can do?

Every time you say yes to something you are using up time and your space that can't be given to something else. You owe it to yourself to be choosy about what you say yes to. When you are able to say no to the wrong things, you have more space to say yes to the right ones, those jobs and opportunities where you get to do your best work and be your best version of yourself. Those are powerful and beneficial opportunities for everyone involved. Think of the people you serve when you are doing your best work.

Taking an opportunity that isn't right for you will stop someone else taking it, someone for whom it might be the perfect work. Something you would slog through and resent, they would sail through and adore. Saying no does them a huge service and saves you huge hassle.

Knowing what to say no to
How do you know what to say no to? You probably know in your heart of hearts the answer to this. Start with those things that you want to say no to but feel like you can't for some reason. For most people it's either not knowing how, or fear of confrontation that stops them saying no in the first place.

How do you know what to say?
Quite often it's simply the mechanics that seem tricky. How do you actually say no? What should you say or not say? Understandably, you don't want to be left with that sinking feeling of letting somebody down that can happen when you say no in an un-empowered way.

There is a way to put down a boundary that can leave you feeling better, not just better from relief but energised and empowered, clear and purposeful. It can be one of the most liberating and empowering experiences if done in the right way.

An Empowered No is positively motivated. It's not confrontation, it's not avoidance, it's not deflection or half truth. It's honest, respectful and straightforward.

A word about sorry
Sorry is a hugely powerful and useful word. The sentiment of apology can show real strength of character. Knowing when we have made a mistake, owning our part in something that hasn't gone well, is important. A heartfelt apology delivered at the right time can repair a relationship, mend a heart and restore faith in a brand. But it's over-used.

For many people sorry has become a modus operandi. You might unconsciously begin sentences with it, emails are littered with it. Some people are practically apologising for even being in the room, sometimes. Whilst it usually comes with the best of intentions, it rarely achieves what you want it to. It can create a feeling of 'wrongness' instead of being an act of generosity, empathy and connection, as it should be. Sorry can reduce the person apologising to a meeker, less empowered version of themselves. It can leave the person receiving it feeling hard done by. Let's reserve sorry for those times when it is really needed and explore the Empowered No and how it is delivered.

An Empowered No is considered. You don't deliver it on the back foot, you give it thought, you prepare for it, build it into your process. You are confident that you are making the right choice.

The first thing that will help you be able to say no is to buy yourself that time to think and build in the expectation in your process that you might say no.

When I coach, I only want to work with the right people, the ones that I can help the most, who I resonate with and who will really value what I can do for them. Rapport is absolutely vital to the coaching relationship and whilst rapport can be built with anyone, it's easier with some than others. That means saying no to quite a few enquiries. I have this built into my process. In my *'what to expect'* PDF that I send out in response to enquiries, it highlights the importance of rapport, of us being the 'right fit', so I know that message has been communicated. In my initial call with the prospective client I clearly set the expectation that we will only work together if I can really be of service. I give myself the time during the call to make that assessment accurately. If I'm sure by the end of the call, I confidently say yes or no. If I'm unsure I can follow up afterwards with a more confident and clear no when I have had time to reflect.

We will explore ways to empower your own process next.

HOW TO SAY NO

Take the time you need to make the right choice Whenever something is asked of you, it's OK to take the time you need to make your decision. You rarely have to respond instantly. Unless you work in emergency services, nothing is really that urgent. Taking that time and delivering the right response first time is way more empowered and respectful of the other person than reflexively saying yes and then having to back track later.

Believe that you are doing the best thing for the other party Saying yes when it's not right for you, is the breeding ground for resentment. Resentment kills the roots from which genuine relationships can grow. You are not serving anyone if you say yes to something knowing you will resent it. It will negatively affect your relationship. You won't do as good a job as you would if you were able to do it joyfully, and the whole experience is a drag for everyone involved.

Saying no is a service when it is the higher integrity choice I had an enquiry from a really lovely prospective client recently. We got on well, I knew I could help her and I was excited about the prospect, but there was also a piece of the puzzle that needed to be in place before we could begin. She needed to do some other work with someone else to be really ready. There was a risk that she might not come back since the other work would be lengthy and expensive, but I knew it was the best option for her. So I said no. Taking her on might have been great for me in the short term and she would have got something from it, but it was even better for her that I said no.

Be clear about what you want Decide before hand if you want to close the door completely or keep it open. This will determine how you phrase your 'no'. Sometimes an opportunity might look great but come at the wrong time, so keeping your options open here makes sense. A continual barrage of requests that are a waste of your time, inappropriate or harassing, are worth closing the door on permanently.

Keep it simple and be clear You don't need a lot of padding or reasons. You can just say *no*.

Don't make excuses It devalues your brand and your integrity. Saying 'I can't make that date' to avoid something rather than simply saying 'no thank you' can get you into uncomfortable territory when dates are flexed to suit you. Avoid 'I'd love to but...' unless of course you would genuinely love to. You may end up having to go through the pain of avoiding something many times over which wastes everyones' time. Avoid using those throw away phrases rather than a straightforward 'no'.

Avoid using time as an excuse Whilst lack of time might be the reason you need to say no to something, you don't need to put it in those terms when you decline an offer. 'I don't have time to...' is rarely received as a valued reason for saying no. Instead what the person hears is 'I'd rather be doing something else or you aren't important enough'. When people say they don't have time, often, although not always, what they really mean is it's not a priority. Of course it's totally fine if something isn't a priority and there are ways of communicating that which will leave a better taste.

Apologise if necessary Check whether an apology is needed. If you are having to break a commitment, then it is by all means appropriate, but often people apologise because they feel they are letting that person down. Here's the rub. They might feel let down, but that's ok. It's not your job to please everyone. You can help them feel better about it by the way you deliver your 'no'.

Phrase it well Avoid using the word 'but'. When you slip a 'but' in the middle of the sentence it reduces its sincerity, and almost wipes out everything that comes before it. 'I really like you but...', 'I'm sure you're an amazing photographer but...', 'I'd love to but...' You can get a sense of how it weakens your message. Just leave it out or replace it with 'and.' Just notice the difference in these two phrases "I'd love to but I don't have time" versus "I'd love to, and when I have more time I will". Which one feels better to deliver and which would you rather be on the receiving end of?

THE EMPOWERED NO, AN EXAMPLE

Things will go a lot better if you speak authentically from the heart, pay attention to your body language, and deliver it at the right pace with appropriate eye contact and tone of voice. With a straightforward no, the person on the receiving end feels respected, and there is no ambiguity about the way forward.

Keeping commitments

You don't have to pull out of commitments already made, nor would I recommend it. Reliability is crucial to your brand and letting people down is never nice. If you do need to extricate yourself, then honesty is always the best policy in my view. Doing it sooner rather than later, giving the other party time to make arrangements, and with a sincere apology is the most respectful and empowered choice. "I'm sorry, I've over committed myself, I need to step down."

Saying no is liberating and gets easier with practice. Finding the turns of phrase that are authentic and natural for you just take a little time and thought. You don't have to say no to everything all at once. You can start slowly and build confidence.

Empowered phrasing

"Thank you so much for the offer…"

"I'm touched that you thought of me…"

"No thank you, it's not for me"

"I'm not able to."

"It doesn't feel right for me."

"It's not right for me at the moment."

THE EMPOWERED NO AT A GLANCE

It is *thoughtfully considered*

You feel *confident* as you know it is the best thing for you *and* the other party

It's *clear and simple* - no excuses, blaming or reasons

It includes the word '*no*'

It rarely includes an apology but may include a *thank you*

It doesn't include a '*but*'

It is delivered *sincerely*, calmly, with good eye contact

AN EMPOWERED PROCESS
a way of working that sets you free

Part of working in an empowered way is to work as efficiently and effectively as you can and to manage the customer journey through your business elegantly and with flair. An Empowered Process is an elegant guided journey that your customers take through the experience of buying from you.

When your process is empowered, you have an opportunity. To do the work you really love, to run your business in a way that liberates you and to enchant your customers every step of the way.

An empowered process is elegant
It's elegant because it's efficient, streamlined and simple. It saves you energy and makes everything easier. It manages the flow of information and keeps your business moving.

It enables you to deal efficiently with enquiries, handle communications at every stage and delight your customer with thoughtful attention to detail.

It's easy to be caught on the back foot, not always knowing how to respond to queries. Wasting time on lengthy conversations and wondering whether cash flow is secure. With an empowered process in place, you won't need to waste effort chasing down invoices or dealing with the same questions time and again but instead preempt challenges and manage expectations clearly and with grace.

An empowered process is a guided experience
It's guided which implies you are in control. You lead your clients where you want them to go.

The journey is an experience. It's not flat and two dimensional, it's carefully considered. You shape the way you want your audience to think and feel. It's an opportunity for you, to build rapport, to showcase your expertise and add value at every turn.

An empowered process makes commercial sense
Having a well thought through process means you won't have offerings competing against each other, so you can increase your reach without decreasing your value.

Having a process that truly works for your business is essential if you are to emancipate yourself to do your very best work.

It means you get to create a way of working that honours what is most important to you, one that prioritises your wellbeing as well as the commercial success of your business and one that makes work the joy it can be.

How many processes do I need?
It makes sense to have a process that works for each offering in your business. Some will be simpler than others depending on the nature of your product or service. If you run an online shop selling homewares, your process will be simpler than an architect seeing a house build through from inception to room styling. Either way, the stages you need to include and the elements you need to manage are likely to be similar.

MAPPING OUT YOUR PROCESS

Consider these as rough headlines when starting to map out a process. For each stage ask yourself what your client needs to know, feel and do, and how you can most effectively and beautifully facilitate that.

The Introduction Where do they first hear of you, how do they learn what you do and why should they chose you? This might be your website, social media platforms, referrals, brochures, flyers or live events.

Enquiries How will you field enquiries? How do you want people to get in touch and what is the first thing they receive from you as a result? You get to manage this. If you don't want enquiries by phone, don't put your phone number on your website or marketing literature. What do they need to know about how you work? This is your first filtering stage. Here's where can set your expectation of pricing and have the opportunity to weed out those people that aren't an ideal fit for your business. This is where a media kit or beautifully presented guide to your business can come in handy.

Vetting If they want to work with you, how do you decide whether you want to work with them? This is essential for service based businesses. You only really want to work with those clients who are ideal. Is it a questionnaire, do you offer an initial call or is a meeting appropriate? This will depend on the scale of the project and the size of the investment they are making. Scheduling a meeting with everyone who thinks they might want to work with you doesn't always make commercial sense, there are other ways to achieve the same result.

Gaining and maintaining commitment This might require a detailed bespoke proposal that gets signed off, it might be a face to face presentation or phone call. It might be simpler. A proposal may or may not be needed depending on how your business operates. How can you make this really compelling and visually beautiful?

The point is you need to demonstrate your expertise, educate your client about what is to come and get a level of commitment before continuing. Maintaining commitment might need to be weaved in more than once throughout your process, particularly if it's a long and complex offering. It helps mitigate post purchase dissonance and keep your clients safely on board.

The welcome They've pretty much committed to working with you/buying from you, how do you make them feel welcome, give them confidence that they have made the right choice and answer key questions they have at this stage?

Delivering your work This might be a simple web transaction with a product shipped in the mail, a face to face presentation of a design project or a workshop. Whatever your work, this is an opportunity to delight, surprise and add value. What needs to happen here that is always part of your process?

Invoicing Where in your process do you need to invoice to ensure cash-flow keeps flowing and to commit the client to the process? Does it help you to have a deposit before beginning work? Would your client prefer to pay in instalments?

Review This stage is often skipped but high performers build it in as a matter of course. Taking time to review for yourself at the end of each project with a very simple, what worked well, what could work better? Mindset can yield plenty of fruit for further improvement.

Follow up Gaining feedback is so valuable and something often forgotten as is a way to say thank you in style. How can you best follow up in a way that is appropriate to your offering and maintaining the relationship?

267

COLLATERAL TO SUPPORT YOUR PROCESS

There are some key pieces of collateral that can really help enhance your process, you might like to consider creating one or all of the following:

* A web-based or mailable *enquiry form*
* An *FAQ's section* on your website or in mailable format
* A *welcome pack* this can be tangible or a more flexible, but still beautifully created, PDF
* A *media kit*, look-book or product brochure
* *A Press Pack*

* *Auto responders* for emails or web enquiries, particularly to manage expectations around response times and next steps
* *Feedback forms*
* *Welcome gifts and thank you gifts* Physical items that come in the mail or online options that add value, whatever works for your brand and your business.

Whatever you send out, they ideally need to be on brand, beautifully presented and well designed so that they add value to your offering and enhance your customer experience.

If the prospect of creating these resources is daunting and you don't want to commission a designer to produce them, I can highly recommend The Brand Stylist *Design for Go Getters* online course, details are in the resources section at the end of the book. In no time you will be skilled up to produce them yourself.

MAKING SURE YOUR PROCESS REALLY WORKS

For your process to truly be an empowering one it needs to be well thought through and work in the context of the bigger picture. You need to keep in mind what's most important. Remind yourself of your values and current priorities. If you are committed to spending more time at home with the family for example, what do you need to build into your process to protect that boundary?

Know your boundaries

If you are designing a new offering, you need to aim for the ideal and define your boundaries. Starting from a place of compromise won't feel empowering and won't yield you the best outcome. When you're crafting your offering know very clearly what you are prepared to do and what it is you are not. This is useful information that you need to make sure you communicate with style. Consider which hours you want to work, how available you want to be. Where does your service begin and end? Will you offer returns or refunds and how will those be managed?

Sense check against your other offerings

Sense check your offering and process with the whole business.

Periodically, for my own company, I list out everything I'm offering, at what price point and for which section of my audience. It helps me see at a glance where things are competing with each other and whether I'm reaching everyone I am aiming at. I will notice where offerings are too close in price or whether there are gaps in who I might be able to serve. This provides a useful springboard for future products or services. I also sense check in relation to time. Noticing how much bandwidth you have for each distinct area of your work and what proportion of revenue it brings in overall will help you determine if it's commercially viable.

WHERE TO FOCUS FIRST

You don't have to overhaul your entire process all at once. It can take a little time to refine and get it right. Producing collateral that works for you is worth doing well. If you are wondering where to start look at your whole business. What currently takes up the most time? What drains your energy? What is driving you nuts? What can you do to address and streamline those areas first?

Once you've streamlined, take a second pass at your process from your clients' perspective. How can you enhance the experience for them? What can you add in or remove at each stage to delight, surprise or add unexpected value?

SOCIAL MEDIA
a conscious approach

If there's one thing that has the potential to get in the way of you getting a job done, it's social media. Don't get me wrong, it's an amazing tool, but it is just that, a tool, not a way of life! You need to take it in hand if you're serious about running an empowered business.

Taking a conscious approach to your social media will be a total game changer for you, I can guarantee it. Whatever the scale of your social media use, making it more deliberate, intentional and outcome driven, will transform your working day.

From careful observation over the years I've noticed there are three main modes of engaging with social media:

The intentional one, the inspiration dip, which is still conscious but less purposeful, and the mindless compulsive one.

In the conscious scenario, you have a clear purpose in mind before engaging. You may have a pre-written post, it might even be part of a scheduled campaign or you are simply inspired in the moment. You are confident, even excited to be putting it out there. It feels good, it feels like positive action. You enjoy the engagement from it. It's often a brief interaction done with efficient ease before you move on to the business of your work.

There's **the inspiration dip** - the check in, if you like. You've got five minutes so you make use of your time by checking on Instagram. How was that last post received? You respond to comments, check out a few profiles and enjoy the inspiration that's out there. It feels productive, you've taken an inspirational dip in the social waters and you're out again ready to crack on with your work.

Then there's **the compulsive interaction**, the mindless one. This is where the comparing mind has the opportunity to show its face and it goes something like this: You find a lull in your productivity so reach for the phone and start scrolling. You go through the motions of checking your profile, the latest likes and comments, a new cat video. There may or may not be much going on, which sends you a

message. There's a niggling feeling. You scroll through your feed. You see what everyone else is up to. You feel the disparity, the gap between your current lull and everyone else's amazingly productive/beautiful/creative/fill in the blank life. Something shifts in your inner landscape. The scrolling becomes a little more mindless, there's very little conscious awareness of what it actually going by.

The whole thing is deeply unsatisfying and does nothing to alleviate the original boredom or drop in productivity. In fact what you are left with is an even greater sense of not doing enough, and even possibly not being enough. When you compound that with having just spent 20 mindless minutes or more achieving nothing, the whole situation feels pretty lame.

We won't get into the whole topic of how addictive social media can be here. For now, what's important is that you take control of the role of social media in your life and in your business.

Social media can be useful for so many things; gaining inspiration, building a tribe, sharing your message, marketing your business, staying connected to a global community, to name but a few. As an Empowered Entrepreneur you just need to be clear about what purpose it is serving for you and give it only the appropriate time and space in your day to efficiently serve that purpose. It is a tool.

When productivity dips, social media is rarely the solution to get you back on track. Far more effective is a burst of fresh air, water or exercise, a creative brainstorm, a change of scene or a break completely. Put social media in its place and recognise when something else is needed to help you get your work done.

GETTING MORE OF WHAT YOU WANT

So often in business we get into a mode of operating that is reflexive, unconscious and just responding to whatever is happening. As an Empowered Entrepreneur you get to have more control and influence over the outcome.

Whether it's how you hold a conversation with a client, craft an email or manage a meeting there are ways to approach things that increases the likelihood of it going well. Let's look at a few scenarios:

An email comes in from a client, they aren't happy, they are clearly upset and making demands that are way beyond what you might be able to accommodate. You feel defensive. They're slinging mud and it's unjustified.

You've engaged a company to provide you with a service, maintaining your website for example. The relationship begins well, but it gradually goes down hill. Over time they take longer and longer to deal with your enquiries, you get the feeling that you're no longer a truly valued customer. On top of all that you begin noticing mistakes, you're losing faith in their competence. It's frustrating, disappointing and an irritation you could do without.

You're approached by someone who really wants to collaborate with you. You aren't sure their business is a good fit for yours. When you dig a little deeper you realise that it would be a wholly unequal partnership and you politely decline. They don't get the message. You are bombarded with requests in different guises. It's draining your time and your energy.

It's easy in these kinds of situation to get rattled, to respond only to the information in front of you and to allow it to consume your time and drain your energy. It can also be easy to fall into allowing the other party to drive what happens, leaving you feeling out of control and disempowered.

Whilst you can't always control external events or the emotional responses of others, you can manage your own reactions and influence things if you take an empowered approach.

EMPOWERING YOUR APPROACH

When a client, friend or relative puts you on the back foot, it can leave you feeling helpless. Here's how to handle the situation in an empowered way.

Take a step back and ask yourself what you want Simply being clear about your ideal outcome makes it much more likely to happen. It shifts your attention towards solutions and enables you to notice favourable opportunities.

Remember it's not personal It can be so easy when feeling under assault to take things to heart and feel like someone has it in for you. I can pretty much guarantee you it won't be personal. Give them the benefit of the doubt, aim to see things from their perspective. It will help you avoid going straight on the defensive and instead see things a more balanced way.

Create the right feeling Taking a moment to think about how you would like the other party to feel will help you moderate your language and approach.

Establish your boundaries Be very clear with yourself about what are you absolutely not prepared to do. This will help you in negotiations. You need to know where you draw the line and at what point you are prepared to step away.

Give yourself time to respond Whilst your gut instinct can be very informative in a situation, it's not always advisable to respond straight off the bat. You also don't need to provide a response immediately just because someone asks for it.

If you need to respond to a tricky situation, draft what you want to say, sleep on it or give yourself time away before reviewing and sending. That said, leaving someone hanging without any acknowledgment of their communication can add fuel to a fire.

Let them know you have their message. Calmly inform them you will be sure to give it careful consideration and come back to them. If someone is badgering you and it's not a priority, you don't have to respond as if it is one. Get to it when it works in your time frame. If you've politely asked them to back off more than once it's OK for them to wait until you have time to give them a considered and respectful response.

Be honest There can be a tendency, particularly in business communication, to be overly formal and operate at a distance. Sometimes a little humanity is what's needed to get the best outcome. As long as you aren't being inflammatory or making accusations, it's perfectly OK to say honestly how you feel.

Choose the right forum We can so easily get drawn into lengthy email conversations or feel put on the back foot in a meeting. Take a moment to consider the most elegant, efficient and empowering way for you to deal with the situation.

Just because someone has sent you an email it doesn't mean you have to reply if scheduling a call with them will get to the heart of the matter quicker. Just because someone catches you unawares in a face to face, it doesn't mean you can't ask them for time to consider and put something in writing. Choose the forum that you feel most comfortable with, that will save you the most time and energy and where you expect to get the best result.

Ask for what you want Knowing what you want is one thing, asking for it is another. Don't expect the other party to be a mind reader. Ask clearly for what you want and give them the opportunity to accommodate.

Remember: Message intended isn't always message received If you get a response you weren't expecting or someone just doesn't get the message, it doesn't mean they are being deliberately cantankerous. Remember it's not personal. Just adjust the way you are communicating and help them get the clarity they need. You may need to do this a few times in different ways. That's OK, keep your cool, just treat it like an opportunity to practice.

Things will not always go your way, in fact if you hit a few roadblocks it's a good sign that you're breaking new ground. Above all, remember, you have what it takes to navigate any situation. Just keep in mind what's most important. Be clear about what you want and keep adjusting your communication and your approach until you get there.

WIN THE MORNING, WIN THE DAY

Setting yourself up for a productive and empowered day can often be a case of starting as you mean to go on.

It may sound bonkers, but if I've made my bed in the morning, I know it's going to be a good day, it's part of my morning routine. A morning routine that reminds you that you are steering your own ship can mean the difference between a day that goes well and one that begins badly and gets worse.

A routine is not a schedule. It's not set by time. Each piece follows on from the one before seamlessly and easily and, if you have to divert from the routine, it doesn't throw everything out of whack, you can just pick it up the next day and start again.

START AS YOU MEAN TO GO ON

A helpful morning routine might look something like this:

Start with awareness and get in the right state

How you feel in your body affects your attitude and your behaviour. Check in with how you feel before you get up and if you're not in a great state, do something to shift it before you move on to anything else. Moving your body will really help, opening the window and taking a few lungfuls of fresh air might be all that's needed. For me the ideal would be yoga and meditation before anything else.

Make your bed

Whatever else happens in your day, making your bed is an instant win. You've already achieved something, albeit small. You have brought order into a little corner of your world. You have started your day with purpose and you have a beautifully made bed to return to at the end of it.

Set your intention

What attitude will you put in the driving seat? Playfulness, curiosity, productivity, peacefulness? Setting that intention to start with makes it more likely to happen and sets the frame for how you will approach things.

Nourish

Good fuel for your body and nourishment for your soul is absolutely essential for productive work. How you eat it matters, too. A bowl of naff cereal hastily guzzled standing at the kitchen counter bent over your phone isn't as nourishing as a freshly prepared breakfast, laid out on the table with flowers, tea in a pot and your favourite music playing.

Orientate

Know your priorities and which direction you are headed in. What are your headline goals? What's first on your agenda? As an Empowered Entrepreneur you get to decide where your focus should be each day. Don't open your emails first thing and let everyone else's priorities become yours. Leave emails until after lunch; there's plenty to do before then.

Create

Creative or strategic client work for me comes first in the day, before the admin and all the other nuts and bolts of running the business happens. Before my head gets clouded with other peoples' thoughts.

This is time to focus, to work from inspiration, to create new work or tackle strategic challenges, and to get away from the laptop or the desk if you can.

As your morning flows into the rest of your day, remember to create space. Take time in nature where you can. Move and nourish your body, change your perspectives, stretch yourself to learn and take on new challenges, assert your boundaries with confidence and get shit done. Enjoy that feeling of steering your ship with purpose. If you find you lose your way, you can just revisit the steps. There's no need to make your bed again but setting an intent, nourishing yourself, re-orientating and creating your valuable work will remind you that you are indeed an Empowered Entrepreneur and you've totally got this.

YOUR JOURNEY STARTS HERE

Well that brings us to the end of our travels through The Empowered Entrepreneur.

It feels like we've explored such a wide landscape. Becoming more intimate with the forces that sustain and lead us, vitality and inspiration. Developing an even greater respect for time, space, nature and for our own abundant capability. Getting more deeply connected to what's important, to our innate wisdom and our capacity for flow. Addressing some fears, some failures and the things that get in the way of getting our work done.

It has been such a privilege to share my perspective and what I've gleaned from my time doing this work. It's been a journey for me in my own life to become more empowered and follow my own authentic path. Shifting the emphasis towards vitality, space, creativity and inspiration in my work have made an immeasurable difference.

I hope this marks the start of a new and wonderful journey for you too. One where you can apply some of the concepts and approaches we've explored to take even more joy, ownership and fulfilment in your work.

It has been such a joy to create this book and I'm so grateful that you have taken the time to read it, thank you!

If you feel inspired, there is more to come. If you would like to explore some of the topics more deeply, you can join me on one of my Empowered Entrepreneur Retreats. There are also plenty of free audios and articles on my blog, and do sign up for my newsletter for details of online courses when they become available. I hope you'll join me and together we can see what unfolds, but for now I wish you every success, whatever that means for you!

Namaste, Elizabeth x

REFERENCES AND RESOURCES

For Empowered Entrepreneur podcasts, stories and resources visit *elizabethcairns.com*

All the beautiful illustrations have been commissioned for this book and are the work of Gail Jones *starkeyslane.com*

For inspirational branding resources including the *Design for Go Getters* online course, and her best-selling books *How to Style your Brand* and *Brand Brilliance*, visit Fiona Humberstone *thebrand-stylist.com*

BOOKS, RESEARCH & INSPIRING PEOPLE MENTIONED IN THE TEXT

Arvay, C (2018) *The Biophilia Effect*, A scientific and spiritual exploration of the healing bond between humans and nature. Sounds True, Boulder.

Pink, D (2018) *When, The Scientific Secrets of Perfect Timing*, Canongate Books. *danpink.com*

Ratey, J J and Manning, R (2014) *Go Wild, Eat Fat, Run Free, Be Social and Follow Evolutions Other Rules for Total Health and Well-Being* Little, Brown and Company.

Michael Ledzion, change maker and chief sportivater, *sportsforschools.org*

Michael Cairns, author and drummer *cairnswrites.com* and *amershammusicstudios.com*

Brene Brown *brenebrown.com* Natural Deodorant Co *naturaldeoco.com* TOMS *toms.co.uk*
Karl Rhonke *karlrohnke.com* Marianne Williamson *marianne.com*

BACH FLOWERS

Many of the illustrations are of plants used to create the Bach Flower Essences. These remedies are a tool for both healing and gaining greater emotional intelligence. For more information visit *healingherbs.co.uk*

PHOTOGRAPHY CREDITS

ANNIE SPRATT 4, 39, 45, 46, 47, 62, 63, 111, 263

CATHY PYLE 1, 13, 20, 27, 33, 35, 57, 61, 69, 87, 91, 104, 106, 116, 123, 131, 144, 146, 150, 153, 160, 170, 175, 189, 209, 211, 226, 228, 279, 280

CECELINA TORNBERG 6, 11, 25, 59, 112, 179, 285

ELIZABETH CAIRNS 2, 15, 73, 84, 109, 137, 159, 167, 190, 192, 196, 197, 203, 207, 218, 221, 235, 237, 264, 282

FIONA HUMBERSTONE 54, 80, 103, 115, 127, 141, 169, 172, 198, 200, 212, 214, 257, 261

KATIE SPICER 9, 42, 49, 50, 95, 249, 269, 275 *and the cover shot*

WITH GRATITUDE

I am so grateful to everyone that has supported me in bringing this book to life.

My editor, husband and hero Mike. Without whom none of it would ever have been remotely conceivable or possible, thank you for your faith in me.

To my darling Smalls. Without you I wouldn't have stepped up and got it done. Your light in my life has made me realise the true power of legacy and living a life of meaning.

To the visionary and brilliant creative whirlwind that is Fiona Humberstone. Your creative direction for the book and constant encouragement as my friend has blown me away. Without you, this would look considerably more shabby ;) You are the nuts!

To dear Gail Jones, thank you for your exquisite and beautiful work on the illustrations and for your encouragement and friendship. I can't imagine this book without your work in it and the care you have taken has touched my heart.

To the amazing photographers who's stunning images grace so many of the pages, Annie Spratt, Cathy Pyle, Cecelina Tornberg and Katie Spicer. You are a joy to work with, true professionals and kindred spirits.

To Duncan, no dream team would be complete without you. Thank you for your sincerity, your incredible work on the videos and for being an all round bloody good egg! To lovely Libby at And Hobbs. Thank you for generously lending us your gorgeous homewares for our styled shoot.

To all the incredible teachers and friends that have been part of my own journey. I am humbled when I think of the privilege it has been to learn from you and that our lives connected when they did. Reg Connolly in particular, a true master of personal empowerment, thank you.

And finally to my clients of the past two decades. Thank you for putting your faith in me and for being a great fit. Thank you for showing up with your whole selves and playing all in. I salute you.

'Ultimately trustworthy and deftly skilled
- the work you do with Elizabeth will last
you a lifetime.'

ZOE HATCH, SONGS OF EVOLUTION

ABOUT THE AUTHOR

As a coach, facilitator, writer and holistic therapist, Elizabeth has worked closely
with hundreds of entrepreneurs in the last 15 years. She understands what it takes to
create a thriving business and live an empowered life.

Her particular passion is working with creative entrepreneurs. Through workshops,
retreats and one to one work, she helps them reconnect with their innate wisdom,
discern what is truly important and create a life of purpose and meaning. She
supports her clients to uncover a more authentic way of working that challenges
conventional norms and breaks the boundaries of what's possible.

Gifted with laser beam insight and an inspirational and sensitive approach, she
brings crystal-clear clarity in moments and holds truly transformational space for
her clients.